ECCLESIOLOGY
IN THE NEW
TESTAMENT

General Editors
Core Biblical Studies
Louis Stulman, *Old Testament*
Warren Carter, *New Testament*

ECCLESIOLOGY IN THE NEW TESTAMENT

E. ELIZABETH JOHNSON

Abingdon Press™

Nashville, Tennessee

Contents

Preface

Several very different churches have shaped who I am. The First Presbyterian Church of Huntington, West Virginia, where I was baptized, nurtured in the Christian faith, and ordained to the gospel ministry formed in me from childhood. The First Presbyterian Church of Athens, Ohio, helped me hold my college study and my Christian faith in conversation and stretched them both, largely in the context of the civil rights movement and the Vietnam conflict, and first encouraged me to consider a theological vocation. The Pilgrim Presbyterian Church of Hamilton, New Jersey (now the United Presbyterian Church in Yardville), the congregation in which I first served as a seminarian; the Covenant Presbyterian Church in Charlotte, North Carolina, where I worshipped while I served as Chaplain at Queens College; the Trinity Presbyterian Church in East Brunswick, New Jersey, where I was married and my children were baptized, who welcomed me as a seminary professor among them; the Reformed Church of North Branch, New Jersey, where my husband served as pastor; and the Central Presbyterian Church in Atlanta, Georgia, which has welcomed many, many seminary professors—have all given me space as a minister to preach, teach, and celebrate the sacraments. Countless other congregations—Baptist and Episcopal, Catholic and Methodist, Pentecostal and Reformed—have invited me into their fellowships over forty years as visiting preacher and teacher and retreat leader, and all of them have taught me about the church.

Parts of this book had their beginnings in the Thomas White Currie Lectures at Austin Presbyterian Theological Seminary, Austin, Texas; the Leckie Lecture Series at First Presbyterian Church, Huntington, West

Virginia; and adult education events at Central Presbyterian Church, Atlanta; Newnan Presbyterian Church, Newnan, Georgia; Saint Luke's Episcopal Church, Atlanta; and Druid Hill Presbyterian Church, Atlanta. I am grateful to all those communities.

Mostly, I am thankful for my family, who endured this work with me and who daily show me what it means to be the church. Peter, Grace, Sarah, and Brandon live out their baptisms with grace and generosity and call me to be faithful to my own. My husband and children are not my only family, though. Kathleen M. O'Connor, Christine Roy Yoder, Martha L. Moore-Keish, and Kimberly Bracken Long, the beloved Pink Lunch group of Columbia Theological Seminary, have read and improved most of this project, and my gratitude to them knows no bounds.

Introduction

In the twenty-first century, the "church," often derisively called "organized religion," is out of favor with many people who consider themselves "spiritual but not religious," or it is ignored as an irrelevant institution of the past. To take up the topic of the church, then—meaning the social or communal character of Christian faith—may seem out of date. That fact makes it all the more important, though, to grapple with the social character of Christian faith as evident first and foremost in the New Testament itself.

The earliest Christians thought of themselves in communal terms. They did not simply make individual personal commitments to Jesus as God's messiah; they constituted themselves as communities shaped by the in-breaking of God's redemptive realm. They likely learned to do so from Jesus himself. When he summoned an inner circle of his followers and numbered them twelve, he signaled that his ministry had the character of a reform movement within Israel. In his work of preaching, healing, exorcism, and prophetic sign actions, Jesus shaped his followers into a particular kind of community that looked like him. After his death and resurrection, his followers already had many pieces of the puzzle that would eventually become what we recognize as the church. N. T. Wright says of the apostle Paul, the earliest Christian writer to whom we have access, that he "regarded the people of God and the Messiah of God as so bound up together that what was true of the one was true of the other. And this becomes in turn the vital key to understanding the close and intimate link" between them.[1]

The English word "church" derives from the Greek *kyriakos*, which means "belonging to the Lord."[2] The word translated "church" in the New Testament, though, is *ekklēsia*, "assembly" or "congregation," and it is used throughout the Greek translation of the Old Testament for the gathered people of God. It is from that word that the term "ecclesiology" arises.

The *ekklēsia* is "the community of those who have been called out [from *ek*, 'out' and *kaleō*, 'I call']." This originally referred to the assembly of the *polis*, or to the citizens who were called to war. The word refers to people being "called out" of their homes and their ordinary life.[3]

Technically, ecclesiology is the study of the nature and mission of the church. Theologians have sometimes simplified the complexity of the New Testament's witness in order to focus on a single image or claim a particular shape for the church. In this study, however, we will highlight diversity and allow the different ecclesiologies in the New Testament to speak in their own voices. This book also investigates New Testament texts about the church from a comparative standpoint. That is, the various authors adopt different metaphors for their communities—*nation, temple, body, family,* and so on—to make differing claims about how they ought to live together and how they ought to live in the presence of God and among their neighbors. Their claims about the nature of the church reflect their understandings of who God is, what God has done in Jesus' death and resurrection, and what the world is and should be. In their descriptions of themselves as the church, early Christians implicitly and explicitly describe also what they believe about biblical Israel, the Jerusalem temple, the Roman Empire, the first-century synagogue, popular philosophical circles, religious and trade associations, and Greco-Roman domestic order and the ways their groups are and are not like those social realities.

There is something both daunting and delightful about a project that cannot help but echo and interact with Paul S. Minear's classic *Images of the Church in the New Testament.*[4] Minear's book became a classic because its extraordinary breadth and depth were governed by a single driving zeal to undergird the work of the twentieth-century ecumenical movement. Indeed, the work sprang from an assignment by the Theological Commission on Christ and the Church of the newly minted World

Council of Churches. The editors of Westminster John Knox Press, in reissuing the volume, pair it with Avery Dulles's *Models of the Church* and say it "remains unparalleled, much less surpassed."[5]

Many things have changed in sixty years, however. Both New Testament studies and the world church are very different phenomena than they were in the middle of the twentieth century. Reflection on metaphor theory, appreciation for the diversity of the New Testament, the growth of interest in the social description of early Christianity, and a substantial reshaping of the ecumenical enterprise, to mention only a few developments, stand between Minear and this project. In particular, rather than urging metaphors for the church to stand in the service of what he considered the most important one—the image of the body of Christ—I intend to hold the various metaphors in conversation with one another. In our own day of ecclesiastical fragmentation and the shift in gravity to the global South, it seems unlikely that a single governing metaphor is helpful for the whole church.

Perhaps one of the more striking changes that have taken place since 1960 concerns who is asking the questions. *Images of the Church* comes from a time when nearly everyone writing about the church in the New Testament looked like Paul Minear, a white man. I do not, and for this reason (among others) I bring a different perspective. The presence of women and people of color in the guild of biblical scholars has profoundly changed the ways we all read the New Testament. That said, I also feel a deep continuity with Minear's theological conception of biblical scholarship, as well as a kinship with him as person. Although I never took a class from him, I knew him and his wife when I was in graduate school and enjoyed many long and fruitful conversations with him. He was the generous kind of Christian scholar, I think, who would not resent my picking up his baton.

What Is the Church?

In the Nicene Creed, an ecumenical statement of faith that dates to 325 CE, Christians affirm that they "believe in one holy, catholic, and apostolic church," but what they believe about that one church varies dramatically from communion to communion. It is not merely that there are Catholic and Orthodox and Protestant churches; there is also great diversity within each of those traditions. That is due in large measure to the wide variety of thinking in the New Testament about the nature and mission of the church and the consequent diversity of interpretations of the New Testament. As Jaroslav Pelikan famously observed, "the history of theology is the record of how the church has interpreted the Scriptures."[6]

A season of uncommonly rapid change, often contentious, among the historic Protestant churches of North America makes this an interesting time to think about ecclesiology in the New Testament.[7] Many people see what can only be termed another reformation going on, much of it prompted by profound disagreements about how Christians read the Bible. There remains a good bit of diversity in the Roman Catholic Church of the twenty-first century too. In these days when increasing numbers of North Americans—particularly young people—describe themselves as "spiritual but not religious," when many distance themselves from religious communities of any sort because they think corporate identity implies restraint of individual freedom, to talk about the church at all is countercultural.[8]

At the beginning of the last century, Alfred Loisy famously said, "Jesus came proclaiming the Kingdom [of God], and what arrived was the Church."[9] There is no reason to think Jesus of Nazareth intended to create a new religion, much less a new institution. As Rudolf Bultmann would later put it, "The proclaimer became the proclaimed."[10] Jesus preached the coming of God's realm, and the church preached Jesus. The church that arose in response to the life, death, and resurrection of Jesus was very much its own creation, although much of that creation owed its inspiration to Jesus and to the traditions of Israel he interpreted. The problem continues to be debated to this day: To what extent can we trace continuity between Jesus and the church that came after him? The problem is the nature of our sources: the twenty-seven books of the New Testament, none of them written during Jesus' lifetime and none by eyewitnesses to his life and ministry; a few other literary references; and a little archaeological evidence.

Luke's sometime name for the church is "the Way" (Acts 9:1-2; 16:17; 18:25-26; 19:9, 23; 24:14, 22). The word also means "road" or "path." It is at once a static image and a metaphor for movement, particularly in light of the travel that pervades the book of Acts. Everyone seems always to be on the road preaching and healing and facing the church's cultured despisers. This is a good reminder that we are dealing with a movement rather than an institution. The Christian groups we identify as churches in the first three centuries of the Common Era gather in people's homes, workplaces, and sometimes even in Jewish synagogues. They may on occasion rent larger spaces to gather several of their groups at a single time, but the overwhelming amount of evidence points to their meeting in homes.[11] The earliest building so far discovered to be used as a church— in the first quarter of the third century—is in Dura-Europos, in present-day Syria. It was originally built as a home to which was later added a meeting hall with a baptistry that was decorated with Christian images.[12] All the earliest Christian communities gather in people's homes, though, so what happens in Dura is a logical extension of the most formative Christian practice.

When they gather, most frequently on "the first day of the week,"[13] in honor of Jesus' resurrection, the early Christians meet to tell stories about Jesus, interpret Israel's scripture, pray to God, exhort one another to live holy and just lives, sing hymns, and share a common meal. Some of their leaders write letters to them that we know are read aloud in their gatherings (see 1 Thess 5:27; Col 4:16), and there is similarly reason to think the Gospels are composed to be read aloud, probably in worship. When perhaps only 5 to 10 percent of people are literate,[14] it is remarkable that we have these twenty-seven documents, composed by anywhere from eleven to seventeen discrete authors, depending on who does the counting, within the space of sixty to seventy years, again depending on who does the counting.

What's a Metaphor For?

Wallace Martin defines a metaphor as "a figurative expression, in which a word or phrase is shifted from its normal uses to a context where it elicits new meanings."[15] The word itself comes from the Greek verb *metapherō*, "I carry away or transfer," because a metaphor transfers aspects of itself to something else. George Lakoff and Mark Johnson argue that metaphors do more than explain one thing in terms of another; they structure the very ways we think.[16] They are not merely descriptive; they are prescriptive. The way we talk about certain things shapes the way we think about them. For instance, in English we talk about "spending time" or "wasting time," which reveals that we use money as a metaphor for time and we think of it in terms of scarcity. A metaphor understands one thing in terms of another such that we see that thing in a new way. The source (the metaphor), added to the target (the thing it describes), forces us to reimagine the target. Frederick Bauerschmidt observes,

> The statement "no man is an island" is both true and a metaphor. That is, no human person is an inert piece of land surrounded by water. On the other hand, though, as the enduring memory of John Donne's words proves, all human beings are connected to all others—or perhaps ought to be.[17]

The image of an island describes the human being in rather specific ways. That is, it deliberately reveals some things and hides others. It hides its character as land rather than human flesh; it reveals its isolation and so discourages the notion that people can or should be isolated from one another. As Beverly Gaventa puts it, "Metaphors ask us to change our minds."[18]

Take for another example what is among the most familiar passages of scripture, the twenty-third Psalm:

> The LORD is my shepherd, I shall not want.
>   He makes me lie down in green pastures;
> he leads me beside still waters;
>   he restores my soul.
> He leads me in right paths
>   for his name's sake.
> Even though I walk through the darkest valley,
>   I fear no evil;
>   for you are with me;

> your rod and your staff—
> they comfort me.
> You prepare a table before me
> in the presence of my enemies;
> you anoint my head with oil;
> my cup overflows.
> Surely goodness and mercy shall follow me
> all the days of my life,
> and I shall dwell in the house of the Lord
> my whole life long. (NRSV)

To say that God is a shepherd hides the facts that God is not a human being and the Psalmist is not a sheep; it reveals, however, that God cares for, guides, protects, feeds, and hosts the Psalmist at a banquet. The metaphor functions to highlight the Psalmist's sense of safety and intimacy with God and to rehearse the Lord's past rescue of the Psalmist from danger.

How different is the picture of God in Isaiah 25:6-8, another picture of God's preparing a banquet:

> On this mountain,
> the Lord of heavenly forces will prepare for all peoples
> a rich feast, a feast of choice wines,
> of select foods rich in flavor,
> of choice wines well refined.
> He will swallow up on this mountain the veil that is veiling all peoples,
> the shroud enshrouding all nations.
> He will swallow up death forever.
> The Lord God will wipe tears from every face;
> he will remove his people's disgrace from off the whole earth,
> for the Lord has spoken.

Here God is described as an Ancient Near Eastern general who celebrates his victory in battle and demonstrates his invincibility by devouring his conquered enemy: "He will swallow up death forever."[19] The two metaphors—shepherd and warrior king—say very different things about Israel's convictions about God. We should neither harmonize nor choose between them because each gives voice to a different experience. As Paul Ricoeur observed, "The symbol gives rise to thought."[20]

So also, when early Christians talk about their communal lives, they use a wide range of metaphors drawn from their religious, civic, social, and cultural heritage. Each of them merits its own consideration. It is this diversity that we explore in this book, not with the intent of unifying or harmonizing these images, but precisely the opposite: to celebrate the richness of scripture's diversity in its witness to the nature and mission of the church.

For Further Reading

Collins, Raymond F. *The Many Faces of the Church: A Study in New Testament Ecclesiology*. New York: Crossroad, 2003.

Küng, Hans. *The Church*. Translated by Ray Ockenden and Rosaleen Ockenden. New York: Burns and Oates, 1968.

Lakoff, George, and Mark Johnson. *Metaphors We Live By*. Second edition. Chicago: University of Chicago Press, 2003; orig., 1980.

Minear, Paul S. *Images of the Church in the New Testament*. Philadelphia: Westminster, 1960.

Williams, David J. *Paul's Metaphors: Their Context and Character*. Peabody, MA: Hendrickson, 1999.

Chapter 1

The People of God: The Church as Israel

Although a real nation named Israel exists both in antiquity and in the present day, in much of the New Testament the biblical nation serves a metaphorical purpose.[1]

Israel as Metaphor

The saga of Israel's beginnings consists of three story cycles about Abraham (Gen 12:1–25:18), his son Isaac (25:19–36:43), and Isaac's son Jacob (37:1–50:26), whom God renames Israel (32:28). God promises Abraham and Sarah, an elderly childless couple, as many descendants as there are stars in the heavens (15:5) and miraculously follows through on the promise. It is a complicated story, though, involving one son, Ishmael, with Sarah's slave woman Hagar, and a second, Isaac, with Sarah herself. Ishmael and Hagar are sent away, and Isaac becomes Abraham's heir. Isaac and his wife Rebekah have two sons as well, Esau and Jacob, and again the younger is the favored one, contrary to Ancient Near Eastern custom. Jacob has twelve sons and one daughter with two wives, Leah and Rachael, and their maidservants Zilpah and Bilhah. The twelve sons become the ancestors of the twelve tribes of Israel, and it seems to be very important that there are twelve of them.

Why twelve? Although scholars do not all agree, it is possible that God's promise to Abraham that his descendants would be as numerous as the stars makes Israelites think about the constellations of the heavens, particularly

1

their "twelveness." There are, after all, twelve months in the year. God's first act of creation is to create day and night—time—which structures all of life in Israel (Gen 1:1-5). Honoring of the Sabbath day is among the ten most important commandments of God (Exod 20:8), rooted in creation itself (Gen 2:2), and Exodus 12 and Leviticus 23 outline in scrupulous detail how Israel is to understand the calendar and its religious obligations. The emergence of the community of the Qumran sectarians in the late first century BCE—the people who write and preserve the Dead Sea Scrolls—arises from a dispute about calendars: the temple establishment of the time uses a solar calendar to schedule offerings, while the traditionalists at Qumran think only a lunar calendar is correct. "Possibly more than any culture, except that of the Chinese, Judaism stresses the observation of patterns in time as a prerequisite for divine favor."[2] Why are there twelve tribes? Perhaps because the world itself is structured around the number twelve.

There are more than twenty lists altogether of the twelve tribes of Israel in the Hebrew Bible, and the names in them do not all agree.[3] Sometimes one tribe is absorbed by another; sometimes a tribe divides; and sometimes the names are simply not the same. Compare only four of the lists: the story of Jacob's sons in Genesis 35:22-26, Jacob's blessing of them in Genesis 49, the census in Numbers 1:20-43, and the blessing of Moses in Deuteronomy 33:

Genesis 35:22-26	Genesis 49	Numbers 1:20-43	Deuteronomy 33
Reuben	Reuben	Reuben	Reuben
Simeon	Simeon	Simeon	Judah
Levi	Levi	Gad	Levi
Judah	Judah	Judah	Benjamin
Issachar	Zebulun	Issachar	Joseph
Zebulun	Issachar	Zebulun	Zebulun
Joseph	Dan	Joseph	Issachar
Benjamin	Gad	Ephraim and Manasseh[4]	Gad
Dan	Asher	Benjamin	Dan
Naphtali	Naphtali	Dan	Naphtali
Gad	Joseph	Asher	Asher
Asher	Benjamin	Naphtali	Jeshurun

It seems as though the names are less important in the long run than the fact that there are twelve of them. The twelve tribes are themselves a metaphor for the people of Israel. Even Ishmael, Abraham's son with Hagar, has twelve sons, "twelve princes according to their tribes" (Gen 25:12-16; 17:20 NRSV). The Essenes at Qumran later adopt the same imagery by constituting their Community Council with twelve members (1QS 8:1).[5]

Through a long series of adventures and misadventures, the confederation of these twelve tribes from roughly the twelfth century BCE—which are constituted by families, clans, and even more complex social arrangements—move from Canaan to Egypt and back again, become a united monarchy in the tenth century under exactly two kings, David and Solomon, and, when the heirs of the second cannot successfully address the problem of succession, divide into two nations. Where the twelve individual tribes of Israel fit in the northern kingdom of Israel and the southern kingdom of Judah is not always clear. In the eighth century, Israel falls to the Assyrian Empire, and in the sixth, Judah is conquered by the neo-Babylonian Empire. The Persian, Greek, and Roman Empires follow them in ruling the little piece of real estate that once was Israel.

By the first century of the Common Era, it has been hundreds of years since Israel and Judah have fallen to the Assyrian and Babylonian Empires, and despite a century of local sovereignty under the Hasmoneans (164–63 BCE) that revives hopes of a restored national entity, the Roman Empire is firmly in charge of what was once the land promised by God to the twelve tribes whose beginnings are recounted in scripture. There is no political Israel; there is instead Palestine, named by the Greeks who invaded it in the 330s BCE, and now a province of the Roman Empire. First-century Palestine is inhabited by Jews, so called because they are from Judea, a variation on Judah. The word *Ioudaioi* can be translated both "Jews" and "Judeans," although the people often still call themselves Israelites.[6] Centuries of warfare and deportation have displaced the people across the known world. They retain their distinctive identity, though, and maintain close contact with the homeland. From the time of the Babylonian Exile and the destruction of the Jerusalem temple in 587 BCE, the traditional religion of Israel begins to be transformed into Judaism—or better, several Judaisms that shape the world of the New Testament. This diversity within first-century Judaism can be best understood by recognizing six important historical shifts that have taken place in the preceding centuries.[7]

1. From the temple to the synagogue. After the Babylonians destroy Solomon's temple in 587 BCE and disperse the elite population, synagogues (the word means "gatherings" or "congregations") begin to be established wherever Judeans and Israelites live. They are as much community centers as places of worship. Synagogue life is marked by prayer and the reading and study of scripture, much of which is being composed and compiled at the time. The interesting thing for our purposes is that synagogues do not disappear after the second temple is built beginning in 516 BCE. Indeed there are synagogues in cities across the entire Roman Empire as well as within Palestine.

2. From Palestine to the Diaspora (the word means "dispersed"). In Jesus' lifetime, there are more Jews living outside Palestine than in it. From 323 to 63 BCE—that is, from the conquest of the land by Alexander the Great to that of Pompey—fully two hundred military campaigns are fought on the territory once ruled by King David. Great numbers of people emigrate or are carried away into slavery. They nevertheless maintain strong ties: family relationships, business dealings, the tax given to support the temple cult, and religious pilgrimages to Jerusalem all keep Jews connected to the homeland whether they live there or not. Diaspora Jews are also inevitably influenced by their non-Jewish neighbors. An important mark of this shift is the translation of the Hebrew Bible into Greek, the *lingua franca* of the Greco-Roman world. The Septuagint (LXX), so named because legend has it that seventy scholars simultaneously made identical Greek translations, is almost always the Old Testament text used by New Testament writers. One of the remarkable aspects of Judaism is its flexibility and accommodation and simultaneous cohesion and distinctiveness. Ritual and monotheism set Jews apart from their neighbors; they resist the religious pluralism of the day, and this is a source of both admiration and resentment among non-Jews.

3. From territorial to religious identity. The word *Jew* originally meant a person from Judea, a geographical or political identity; by the first century CE it means instead a devotee of a specific cult. The religion of Israel has become Judaism in the centuries since the Exile. It has become portable, marked by a distinctive lifestyle rather than geographic location or even the operation of the temple cult. Jews define themselves by their devotion to God and God's law. They are known by their neighbors for particular facets of that devotion, particularly circumcision, Sabbath observance, and table fellowship. Both their food practices and their commitment to honor the Sabbath make it impossible for Jews to serve in the army, so they are frequently exempted from military service. Non-Jews find circumcision to be barbaric and frequently ridicule it, and they think that the reason Jews abstain from pork is that their god is a pig. Nevertheless, some non-Jews, particularly those of Stoic persuasion, find Jewish monotheism philosophically attractive, and we find thriving Jewish missionary ventures throughout the first century.[8] Throughout the New Testament and Second Temple Jewish literature we see God-fearers—non-Jews who worship the God of Israel—and proselytes or converts to Judaism.[9] The Wisdom of Solomon, a piece of Jewish literature from the period between the late first century BCE and the early first century CE, is at least partially addressed to non-Jews.

4. From the temple cult to the study of scripture. One consequence of the destruction of Solomon's temple is the writing down of traditions. A people in exile retains its continuity with the past by telling and interpreting its stories. By the time of Jesus, Jews have become a people of the book. This is why it is impossible to understand the New Testament without knowing the Old Testament. In the New Testament we find nearly every writer interpreting the Bible as they reflect on their Christian lives and communities. Similarly, the charter of the Qumran community says that at all times of the day and night there are to be at least ten men engaged in the study of scripture.[10]

5. From priestly to lay leadership. The formation of scripture fosters a class of people learned in it, known variously as scribes and lawyers, who are closely associated with the Pharisaic party, a lay movement that seeks to bring temple purity into the home. The Pharisees are the first people to think in terms of what the Protestant reformers would later call the priesthood of all believers.[11] They are particularly concerned with family, food, and agricultural practices, but they believe there is no area of human life about which God does not care, so they engage in extensive exegesis of the Bible to learn what God wants.[12] Pharisaic teachers are often addressed as *rabbi*, "my master." Prior to 70 CE, though, that is an honorific title; after 70 it becomes a technical term for someone trained by another rabbi. Consequently, post-70 Judaism is often called rabbinic Judaism. It is important here to remember that the first generation of Christianity is before 70, but all New Testament writers except one— Paul—write after 70. This makes the use of rabbinic literature, itself not written down and codified until the second through the fourth centuries CE, a bit problematic although sometimes helpful for reading the New Testament.

6. From diversity to uniformity: the significance of 70 CE. All these shifts are well underway before 66–70, when a rebellion against Rome erupts in Palestine and is violently quashed. The Romans burn the temple in Jerusalem and march Jewish prisoners of war through the streets of Rome. In 135 Simon Bar Kochba seeks to reverse the tide of history, starts yet another rebellion, and makes matters even worse. The partially restored Jerusalem is leveled and renamed Aelia Capitolina. The Romans sow salt on the ground so that nothing will even grow there.[13] Many Jews, though, are able religiously to survive the failed rebellions. Judaism endures because some Jews have learned to live without the temple before it is destroyed. Prior to 70, we hear of many groups of Jews: Pharisees, Sadducees, Essenes, Zealots, and Jewish Christians; there were probably others of whom we know nothing. Only two groups are visible after the revolts, though—the Pharisees and the Christians. Pharisees become the dominant force after 70 and Pharisaic Judaism becomes "normative" Judaism, although there continues to be enormous diversity among Jews.

An influential source of authority at the end of the first century is located in the rabbinic academy at Jamnia, about thirty miles from Jerusalem near the Mediterranean coast, headed by a Patriarch who is

> In the days to come
> the mountain of the LORD's house
> will be the highest of the mountains.
> It will be lifted above the hills;
>   peoples will stream to it.
> Many nations will go and say,
> "Come, let's go up to the LORD's mountain,
> to the house of Jacob's God
>   so that he may teach us his ways
>   and we may walk in God's paths." (Isa 2:2-3)

Isaiah's vision gives voice to a long-held conviction in Israel. From the beginning of time, Adam is created by God to be not only the ancestor but also the caretaker of the whole world (Gen 2:4-15), and the patriarch Abraham's commission is to be a blessing to all the nations (Gen 18:18; 22:18; 26:4). Israel's vocation has always been for the sake of the whole world. Jesus embodies this vocation not by reaching out himself to non-Jews, but by crossing significant religious and cultural boundaries within Judaism, thus setting a precedent for his followers. Jesus repeatedly eats with tax collectors and sinners, he touches dead bodies and lepers, and he engages women in serious conversation in public, all violations of proper religious behavior. The church's eventual move to include Gentiles is in keeping with both the prophetic vision and Jesus' practice.

The Spirit then casts Jesus out[22] into the wilderness for forty days (Mark 1:12-13), which recalls the twelve tribes' wandering in the wilderness for forty years (Exod 16:35).[23] Jesus and Satan size each other up as enemies on the battlefield. The word translated "tempted" in verse 13 is better rendered "tested" here, because not a word is exchanged between them, as in Matthew's and Luke's stories,[24] and what Satan and Jesus do is test each other's mettle as opponents. Each is arrayed with his troops: Satan has the demons who will populate the first part of Mark's book, and Jesus has wild animals and angels. He will soon add to that army human soldiers.

In the next paragraph Jesus walks up to two pairs of brothers who are described as "fishers," Simon and Andrew and James and John, and calls them to "follow me and I will make you to become fishers of human

9

beings" (1:17 author translation).[25] Remarkably, they respond positively to Jesus' summons, leave their family fishing businesses, and follow Jesus as he embarks on a mission of preaching, healing, and exorcism.

"Such a peremptory call issued by a teacher to an unsuspecting bystander or member of the audience is not known among Jewish teachers around the time of Jesus or even in the later rabbinic period," says John Meier. "It was, in general, the later rabbinic custom for a student to seek out a teacher. Jesus' style harks back instead to the prophet Elijah calling Elisha [1 Kgs 19:19-21]."[26] The popular philosophers of the day—more like self-help gurus or life coaches than academic philosophers—also generally wait for students to seek them out. Jesus is different. John the Baptist seems to have disciples, as Jesus does, although we know nothing of how he collects them (Matt 9:14; Mark 2:18; 6:29; Luke 5:33; John 3:25). In view of the fact that Jesus takes after John in other respects, it is possible that John similarly summons his disciples and they accompany him.

After Mark tells several stories of exorcisms and healings, he has Jesus again call someone to "follow me," this time a tax gatherer named Levi (2:13-14). No further disciples are named until 3:13, when there is a larger group with an inner circle that numbers twelve:

> He went up the mountain and summoned to him those whom he himself wished, and they came to him. And he made Twelve in order that they might be with him and that he might send them out to preach and to have authority to cast out demons. And he made the Twelve and gave the name *Petros* to Simon; James son of Zebedee and John the brother of James he gave the name *Boanergēs* to them, that is, "Sons of Thunder"; and Andrew, and Philip, and Bartholomew, and Matthew, and Thomas, and James son of Alphaeus, and Thaddaeus, and Simon the Cananaean, and Judas Iscariot, who betrayed him. (3:13-19a)[27]

Several things bear noting here. As in the earlier stories of Simon, Andrew, James, John, and Levi, those whom Jesus calls in chapter 3 follow him in order that they might be with him (v. 14), leaving behind hearth and home.[28] The first sentence describes Jesus' gathering a group from which he "makes" the Twelve. Levi is not on the list. Are we to take "Matthew the tax collector" in Matthew 10:3 to be the Matthew of Mark 3:18? Christian tradition thinks so, and explains that Levi's name has changed, even though his line of work has not. It is instead more likely that in Mark Levi is a member of the larger circle of people who follow Jesus rather than one of the Twelve. As we will see, the lists of the Twelve do not all contain the same names.

Three of the men—Simon, James, and John—who appear together as a trio repeatedly in the rest of Mark's book are given symbolic names.[29] Peter is a common name today, but in antiquity no one before this man was named *Petros*, which means "rock." Perhaps it is analogous to the modern nickname "Rocky," which was famously given to a Hollywood prizefighter.[30] Does Jesus mean that Peter is as hard as a rock? Certainly Mark's portrayal of him does not describe an unfeeling man. Does the rock instead signify his steadfastness or solidity? If so, few of the stories about Simon in Mark's Gospel bear that out. It is not clear what the sobriquet means. From this point forward in the narrative, though, Simon will be referred to as Peter, with the notable exception of 14:37, where his loyalty to Jesus is in doubt.[31] The sons of Zebedee Jesus calls "Sons of Thunder." The phrase *epethēken onoma* in verse 16, literally "he added a name," suggests the granting of a family name, much as in a legal adoption an adoptive father gives his family name to an adoptee.

The apostle Paul—who writes his letters before the Gospels are composed—knows Simon only by this nickname, although he uses the Aramaic word for "rock," *Cephas*, more frequently than the Greek *Petros*.[32] John 1:42 similarly identifies Simon as *Cephas*, translates that to mean *Petros*, and notes that both words mean "rock." In Matthew 4:18, the first time Jesus meets Simon in that book, he is already "called Peter" with no explanation of how that has come to be; and at Luke 5:8, the first appearance of Simon in that Gospel, he is referred to as Simon Peter, also with no comment. Although Matthew offers an explanation for Jesus' renaming Simon Peter as the rock on which the church is to be built (Matt 16:15-19), that is clearly after the fact, since Peter has been his name since he entered Matthew's story. In Mark, there is no explanation at all of why Simon gets his nickname, simply a statement that Jesus confers it.

The early church knows Simon almost exclusively as Peter. He is a major character in the first half of the book of Acts and appears throughout the church's tradition as the founder of Christianity in Rome and a martyr of the faith.[33]

"Sons of Thunder" is another suggestive nickname. Some interpreters have suggested that it recalls the heavenly voice that identifies Jesus as God's son at 9:7,[34] but like "Rocky," it could also carry intimations of the cosmic battle looming in the advent of Jesus.[35] The nicknames seem to be more about who the men will become than who they already are. Rocks and thunder are forceful images, reminding Mark's reader of Jesus' squaring off against Satan in the wilderness where the two adversaries size each other up before battle, each in the company of his soldiers (1:12-13). This is not a war between human opponents but cosmic ones: Jesus casts out the satanic powers and gives these men power to exorcise as well (3:15; compare 6:7, 13). Why only three of the Twelve receive symbolic names is not clear, although it is telling that Jesus bestows them rather than their arising, as nicknames so often do, from within the group.

The last person in the list is called "Judas Iscariot, who betrayed Jesus" (3:19a), despite the fact that, to this point in Mark's story the narrative has not said that Jesus will be betrayed by anyone.[36] Judas is described as "one of the Twelve" also at Matthew 26:14, 47; Mark 14:10, 20, 43; Luke 22:3, 47; and John 6:70-71, a remarkably consistent identification. John Meier argues persuasively that this identification of Judas with the Twelve is among the strongest pieces of historical evidence that the Twelve actually existed as Jesus' inner circle, since it is scandalous both to early Christians and to their cultured despisers that Jesus is handed over to death by a friend, a claim the Gospel writers would surely have had no incentive to make up.[37] The phrase "the Twelve" occurs a total of thirty-five times in the New Testament, twenty-four of those not modifying a word like "disciples" or "apostles.[38] Clearly it is a well-known title for Jesus' inner circle.

One of the more historically certain things we know about Jesus of Nazareth is that he has disciples. The word *mathētēs*, which comes from the verb "I learn," occurs 253 times in the New Testament, all of them in the Gospels and Acts. It refers generally to people who follow Jesus, and sometimes specifically to the Twelve of his inner circle.[39] Although some scholars dismiss the Twelve as a later projection of the church onto Jesus,[40] there are numerous reasons to resist such skepticism. Their existence is multiply attested,[41] and the fact that Judas is identified as one of them is an embarrassment to the church—and as such a sure indicator that we are dealing here with historical fact rather than later interpretation.

This leaves us with a consistent picture of Jesus' inner circle described as the Twelve but with a thoroughly inconsistent list of names numbering not twelve but eighteen.

Matt 10:2-4	Mark 3:16-19a	Luke 6:13-16	Acts 1:13b	John
Simon Peter	Simon Peter	Simon Peter	Peter	Simon Peter
James of Zebedee	James of Zebedee	James of Zebedee	James of Zebedee	James of Zebedee
John of Zebedee	John of Zebedee	John of Zebedee	John of Zebedee	John of Zebedee
Andrew	Andrew	Andrew	Andrew	Andrew
Philip	Philip	Philip	Philip	Philip
Bartholomew	Bartholomew	Bartholomew	Bartholomew	
Matthew	Matthew	Matthew	Matthew	
Thomas	Thomas	Thomas	Thomas	Thomas
James of Alphaeus	James of Alphaeus	James of Alphaeus	James of Alphaeus	
Thaddaeus	Thaddaeus			
Simon of Cana	Simon of Cana	Simon the Zealot	Simon the Zealot	
Judas Iscariot	Judas Iscariot	Judas Iscariot	Judas	Judas Iscariot
		Judas of James	Judas of James	Judas not Iscariot
			Matthias	
				Nathanael
				Beloved Disciple

Although John's Gospel does not list the names of the Twelve as the other three Gospels do, and despite the fact that it knows there are twelve of them (John 6:67, 70-71; 20:24), it refers to only ten by name. Simon Peter, Judas, and Thomas are explicitly identified as members of the group (John 6:66-71; 20:24), and Nathanael of Cana, the sons of Zebedee, "and two others of his disciples" are with them when the risen Jesus arrives for breakfast on the beach (21:2 NRSV). The call of Philip is narrated at 1:43. Andrew is three times identified as Peter's brother (1:40, 44; 6:8). The mysterious "disciple whom Jesus loved,"[42] who is never named (scholars have dubbed him the Beloved Disciple), is present also at table the night Jesus is betrayed (13:23), shares Peter's resurrection appearance (20:2), and stars in the final paragraph of the book (21:20-23).

Simon Peter, James and John of Zebedee, Andrew, Philip, Thomas, and Judas Iscariot appear in all four Gospels and Acts. John does not name Bartholomew, Matthew, or James the son of Alphaeus. Matthew and Mark know Thaddeus but not Judas the son of James who is in Luke and Acts. Nathanael of Cana is one of the Twelve only in the Fourth Gospel, as is the Beloved Disciple. Simon Peter is named fully 177 times in the New Testament, not only in the Gospels and Acts but also in 1 Corinthians and Galatians, and he is called variously Simon, Simon Peter, Peter, and Cephas. One letter, 1 Peter, is written by someone apparently named for him, and another letter, 2 Peter, purports to have been written by him, although that is highly doubtful, since it comes from a later generation. By contrast, Simon's brother Andrew makes only thirteen appearances. James and John the sons of Zebedee show up much more frequently, notably including the story of James's death at the hands of Herod (Acts 12:2), although John disappears from Luke's story after the list in Acts 1:13. Philip is much more prominent in John's Gospel than he is in the Synoptics,[43] as is Thomas. Bartholomew is named only in the four lists. Matthew appears five times, as does James the son of Alphaeus; Thaddeus, Simon the Zealot, and Simon the Cananean twice each. Both Luke and John say there is a second Judas, not Iscariot. Judas Iscariot is named seventeen times.

Luke goes to great lengths in Acts 1:16-26 to say that Judas Iscariot—whose death is described variously in Matthew 27:5 and Acts 1:18—must be replaced so that the eleven disciples will again become the Twelve:

"Brothers and sisters, [says Peter after Pentecost] the scripture that the Holy Spirit announced beforehand through David had to be fulfilled. This was the scripture concerning Judas, who became a guide for those who arrested Jesus. This happened even though he was one of us and received a share of this ministry." (In fact, he bought a field with the payment he received for his injustice. Falling headfirst, he burst open in the middle and all his intestines spilled out. This became known to everyone living in Jerusalem, so they called that field in their own language Hakeldama, or "Field of Blood.") "It is written in the Psalms scroll,

> *Let his home become deserted and let there be no one living in it;*

and

> *Give his position of leadership to another.*

"Therefore, we must select one of those who have accompanied us during the whole time the Lord Jesus lived among us, beginning from the baptism of John until the day when Jesus was taken from us. This person must become along with us a witness to his resurrection." So they nominated two: Joseph called Barsabbas, who was also known as Justus, and Matthias. They prayed, "Lord, you know everyone's deepest thoughts and desires. Show us clearly which one you have chosen from among these two to take the place of this ministry and apostleship, from which Judas turned away to go to his own place." When they cast lots, the lot fell on Matthias. He was added to the eleven apostles.

Why are the names of the Twelve so inconsistent? If it is so important to have twelve men that Judas must be replaced, why does Matthias promptly disappear from Luke's story without another mention of him? Only Simon Peter, James, John, Judas, Thomas, Philip, Nathanael, and the Beloved Disciple have any significant roles in the Gospel narratives; the other men show up for the most part only in lists or in passing. What seems to matter most—as with the lists of the tribes of Israel—is their "twelveness"[44] rather than their individual identities. Furthermore, most of the Twelve "disappear with surprising rapidity" after the first Easter.[45]

Jesus brings into being a community around himself that is a reformed and reforming Israel.[46] Matthew 19:28 seems key here. "Jesus said to them, 'Truly I tell you, at the renewal of all things, when the Son of Man is seated on the throne of his glory, you who have followed me will also sit on twelve thrones, judging the twelve tribes of Israel'" (NRSV; compare Luke 22:30). Nowhere else in Jewish literature do we find a picture of twelve human beings sharing God's prerogative of eschatological judgment.[47] "Jesus created the group called the Twelve, whose very number symbolized, promised, and (granted the dynamic power thought to be present in the symbolic actions of prophets) began the regathering of the twelve tribes."[48] The Twelve function vicariously for the whole people of God.[49] What we learn about Jesus and the Twelve is that he gathers them and sends them out. Their mission is restricted to "lost sheep of the house of Israel," as is Jesus' own (Matt 10:6 NRSV; 15:24) until after Easter, when it is extended to "all nations" (28:18). The inclusion of the Gentiles, reaching beyond the Israel of the twelve tribes, is a sign of the coming of God's victory and the redemption of the whole world.

This community Jesus calls into being is marked by porous boundaries, unconventional practices, and radical commitment to the least, the lost, and the last. God's redemption of the world is breaking in around Jesus, signaled by his authority over demons, his healing of sick people, and his other works of power. By reaching out specifically to people considered religiously unclean and sinful and welcoming them—the tax collectors and prostitutes who populate the Gospels—Jesus sets the agenda for the church that follows him.

The image of Israel in the image of the Twelve cannot refer literally to the twelve tribes, since the disciples Jesus summons do not individually represent each of those tribes. Two pairs of brothers alone are enough to prevent the men from having descended one each from Jacob's twelve sons. They instead point beyond themselves to the restoration of the people of God and the vindication of God's sovereignty over the whole earth. One of the more remarkable developments in early church history is how soon the Jews who believe in Jesus reach out to non-Jews. Within a matter of a very few years, we find whole communities of Christians who once were pagans of varying sorts, as well as congregations that include both Jews and Gentiles. Once the church begins to include many non-Jews, the church as Israel becomes a frequently fraught metaphor. It is contested in the apostolic age and even more hotly so in the postapostolic age.

For Further Reading

Meier, John P. *A Marginal Jew: Rethinking the Historical Jesus*. Five volumes. New York: Doubleday, 1991–2016.

Chapter 2

A Fraught Metaphor: "New" Israel and "True" Israel

There are vastly different and competing views of just how the church is to be seen as Israel in the New Testament.[1] The first Christian writer we know, Paul, frequently refers to the Christian communities he founds in terms borrowed from Israel, although he invariably maintains the separate identities of Jews and Gentiles, even within the church:

> Jews ask for signs, and Greeks look for wisdom, but we preach Christ crucified, which is a scandal to Jews and foolishness to Gentiles. But to those who are called—both Jews and Greeks—Christ is God's power and God's wisdom. This is because the foolishness of God is wiser than human wisdom, and the weakness of God is stronger than human strength. (1 Cor 1:22-25)

The proclamation of the gospel message is for both Jews and Gentiles, and it offends both even as it offers salvation to both. Although Paul says he and Peter divide the mission field—"I had been given the responsibility to preach the gospel to the people who aren't circumcised, just as Peter had been to the circumcised" (Gal 2:7)—the word of God is the same to each. Significantly, though, and differently from many other New Testament writers, Paul insists that Gentiles do not convert to Judaism when they become Christians.

In Romans 9–11 Paul engages in the most sustained and nuanced theological reflection on the relationship between the church and Israel in the New Testament. He argues that God's impartial treatment of Israel and the nations (the meaning of the word *Gentiles*), reaching out to both in sovereign mercy and calling both to trust the faithfulness of Jesus Christ, will never nullify God's covenant faithfulness to Israel. God is absolutely impartial and enduringly faithful. God calls both Jews and Gentiles because of who God is, not because of people's worthiness, and it is Christ's faithfulness to God rather than people's faithfulness to God's covenant that rescues the human race from the powers of sin and death. Remarkably, he claims that the Gentiles' positive response to Christian preaching, compared with the somewhat less enthusiastic reception among Jews, is in fact God's way of ensuring the redemption of "all Israel" (Rom 11:26).[2] The advantage Israel has by having been entrusted first with God's covenant is balanced by God's "hardening" (9:18; 11:7, 25) part of Israel in order to make an opportunity for Gentiles to respond to the gospel, which response will provoke Israel to jealousy and, apparently, to faith. His final benediction in Galatians asks God's blessing on both the Christian church and "the Israel of God" (Gal 6:16 NRSV).[3]

Matthew, on the other hand, thinks of the church as the "new" Israel that replaces Jews who do not believe in Jesus. Matthew's Jesus says his followers' righteousness must exceed that of the scribes and Pharisees (5:17-20), and he repeatedly portrays Jesus teaching in "their synagogues"[4] as though to underscore the difference between them and Matthew's own synagogue peopled by Jews who believe in Jesus. The cause of Matthew's conflict with Jews who do not believe in Jesus is the competition between his church and the non-Christian synagogue for converts (23:15). We see this most clearly in chapter 23.

> Then Jesus said to the crowds and to his disciples, "The scribes and the Pharisees sit on Moses' seat; therefore, do whatever they teach you and follow it; but do not do as they do, for they do not practice what they teach. They tie up heavy burdens, hard to bear, and lay them on the shoulders of others; but they themselves are unwilling to lift a finger to move them.... But woe to you, scribes and Pharisees, hypocrites! For you lock people out of the kingdom of heaven. For you do not go in

yourselves, and when others are going in, you stop them. Woe to you, scribes and Pharisees, hypocrites! For you cross sea and land to make a single convert, and you make the new convert twice as much a child of hell as yourselves." (23:1-4, 13-15 NRSV)

Most of Matthew's vitriol is reserved for the Pharisaic leadership and the temple establishment, but after Pilate pronounces Jesus innocent of any crime, the people as a whole say, "Let his blood be on us and on our children" (27:24-25). When at the end of Matthew's book the risen Jesus commissions the eleven (Judas has died at this point) to "go and make disciples of all nations," the reader is left to wonder whether or not historic Israel is part of "all nations."

The Fourth Gospel similarly treats the church as the "true" Israel that replaces the synagogue.[5] Although the community to which John's Gospel is addressed is overwhelmingly Jewish in composition,[6] the evangelist manifests great hostility toward Jews who do not believe in Jesus. Whereas the other evangelists talk about Pharisees, Sadducees, and temple officials, John much more frequently lumps them all together into a single group he calls "the Jews," almost equivalent to "the world" that is hostile to Jesus and persecutes his friends.[7] He says Jews who reject Jesus are unable to understand scripture (John 5:39-40), claims they are not children of God but of Satan (8:44), and even accuses them of idolatry. The crowd at Jesus' trial shouts, "We have no king but the emperor" (19:15 NRSV) on the eve of the Passover, during which they will say, "We have no king but God." John's church has been excluded from the synagogue (9:22; 12:42; 16:2) and apparently some members have even died in the ensuing conflict (16:2).[8] Although this is a far more serious dispute than we find in Matthew, it results in a very similar redefinition of Israel, this time based not on competition for members—a question of ecclesiology—but on Christology, that is, the identity of Jesus.

In Hebrews as well, the church is the "true" Israel that replaces the synagogue. A primary aim of the treatise is to demonstrate the immeasurable superiority of Christianity over Judaism. "In the past, God spoke through the prophets to our ancestors in many times and many ways. In these final days, though, he spoke to us through a Son" (1:1-2).

21

"Jesus has become the guarantee of a better covenant" than the one given through Moses (7:22). "But now, Jesus has received a superior priestly service just as he arranged a better covenant that is enacted with better promises. If the first covenant had been without fault, it wouldn't have made sense to expect a second" (8:6-7). Here again, as in Matthew, there seems to be a measure of competition between two communities of Jews, one that believes in Jesus and one that does not, since the author chides those who "stop meeting together with other believers" (10:25). The word "meeting together" there, *episynagōgēn*, is related to the word "synagogue" and describes those who worship with the (non-Christian) synagogue rather than with the Christian community.

Despite the common observation that the name of Jesus appears in James only at 1:1 and 2:1, there is no doubt that this letter is addressed to Christians. Its salutation reads "From James, a slave of God and of the Lord Jesus Christ. To the twelve tribes who are scattered outside the land of Israel. Greetings" (1:1). This description of the church as "the twelve tribes in the Diaspora"[9] is a most explicit use of the nation of Israel to describe the church. Although the letter is clearly written to Jewish Christians, "Israel" is still a metaphor here because there are many other Jews who do not believe in Jesus. James belongs with those Christians who think the church is the "true" Israel.[10] The function of the metaphor is to reinforce community boundaries and to exhort the recipients to live lives defined by the law of God and remain single-minded in their devotion.

First Peter is addressed to Christian groups in Asia Minor that are composed of Gentile believers who are members of pagan households and being harassed and derided by their families and friends for their refusal to participate in their common religious life. In response, the author uses all kinds of biblical language to describe them with epithets originally used for Israel. They are "exiles of the Dispersion" (1:1 NRSV; compare 2:11) and "the flock of God" (5:2-3) of whom Jesus is "the chief shepherd" (5:4; compare Ps 23:1). The word "Gentiles" is used in 1 Peter to identify not non-Jews but non-Christians (2:12; 4:3). Most importantly, 1 Peter piles up Bible verses about Israel's relationship with God to praise and encourage these Gentile Christian women and slaves who live in a hostile environment.

> But you are a chosen race, a royal priesthood, a holy nation, a people who are God's own possession. You have become this people so that you may speak of the wonderful acts of the one who called you out of darkness into his amazing light. Once you weren't a people, but now you are God's people. Once you hadn't received mercy, but now you have received mercy. (1 Pet 2:9-10)

Pieces of Isaiah 43:20 ("chosen people"), Exodus 19:6 ("priestly kingdom and a holy nation"), Hosea 1:9 ("not my people"), and Hosea 1:6 ("no compassion" or "no mercy") that originally denote Israel are woven together and applied to Gentile Christians.[11] Here the metaphor serves a pastoral function, what Steven Bechtler calls the "revalorization of shame."[12] First Peter takes the lowly and shameful status of Christians who are scorned and ridiculed by their kinfolk and neighbors and turns it into honor of which they can be proud.

In Revelation 7, John of Patmos sees a vision of 144,000 Christians vindicated by God after having suffered martyrdom at the hands of the Roman Empire. Each of the tribes of Israel is represented by twelve thousand members.

> Then I heard the number of those who were sealed: one hundred forty-four thousand, sealed from every tribe of the Israelites:
>
>> From the tribe of Judah, twelve thousand were sealed;
>>
>> from the tribe of Reuben, twelve thousand;
>>
>> from the tribe of Gad, twelve thousand;
>>
>> from the tribe of Asher, twelve thousand;
>>
>> from the tribe of Naphtali, twelve thousand;
>>
>> from the tribe of Manasseh, twelve thousand;
>>
>> from the tribe of Simeon, twelve thousand;
>>
>> from the tribe of Levi, twelve thousand;
>>
>> from the tribe of Issachar, twelve thousand;
>>
>> from the tribe of Zebulun, twelve thousand;

from the tribe of Joseph, twelve thousand;

from the tribe of Benjamin, twelve thousand were sealed. (7:4-8)[13]

Each of these people "who had been slaughtered on account of the word of God and the witness they had given" (6:9) is marked on the forehead with God's own seal. A seal is evidence of a king's property and authority.[14] The repetition—"from the tribe of Reuben, twelve thousand; from the tribe of Gad, twelve thousand," and so on—signals that we are dealing here with liturgy, the language of worship, perhaps even a hymn. It is almost a roll call. That the martyrs are identified as being from the twelve tribes of Israel is telling, since the evidence elsewhere in Revelation suggests that the Christians to whom the book is addressed are not all Jews by any means. Asia Minor, which is where they live, does indeed have many Jewish communities, but what we know of the churches in Ephesus, Smyrna, Pergamum, Thyatira, Sardis, Philadelphia, and Laodicea suggests that they are of mixed composition. In Smyrna and Sardis they face hostility from "Satan's synagogue," people who say they are Jews but are not (2:9; 3:9), probably signifying that they are Jews who do not believe in Jesus. In Ephesus, Pergamum, and Thyatira there are Christians who believe they may eat meat that has been slaughtered in pagan temples and sold in the market (2:14, 20), a practice that we know that Paul finds acceptable so long as it does not encourage idol worship (1 Cor 8:1–11:1). We also know that Jewish Christians—other than Paul—would not engage in it (compare Acts 15:29). In Ephesus and Pergamum these people are called Nicolaitans (2:6, 14).[15] Although the seer roundly condemns them, they clearly consider themselves to be Christians and are tolerated by at least some other Christians. Such diversity of faith and practice among Christians is very much the order of the day in early Christianity, as Paul's letters repeatedly bear witness. For our purposes, the debate about idol meat demonstrates that not all the people in the churches to which Revelation is addressed are Jews. What, then, is the effect of describing the church as the twelve tribes of Israel sealed with God's own seal?

The answer concerns both proper ethics and the shoring up of community boundaries. Faithful Christians, from the seer's perspective, as the restored people of Israel, keep the law of God as given to Moses

24

and interpreted by Jewish Christians like John. They honor the food and table fellowship laws written in the Bible and rooted in Jewish tradition. They avoid sexual immorality as the Bible defines it. Furthermore, they are to be distinguished not only from pagans who dishonor God by worshipping idols and who persecute the church but also from those who call themselves either Jews or Christians but whose life and worship are different from John's. The metaphor of Israel here stands in the service of religious and moral exhortation and the maintenance of community boundaries.

The Dangers of Supersessionism

Jeffrey Siker traces the figure of Abraham as the father of Christians, borrowed from the Bible, throughout the New Testament and the postapostolic period. Paul claims in the first generation of the church that Gentiles who believe in Jesus become Abraham's children and thus are included with Jews in Israel (Rom 4:1-15; 9:7-13; Gal 3:6-9, 29). By the time of Justin Martyr's *Dialogue with Trypho the Jew* in the second century, though, only Christians are considered Abraham's children and Jews who do not believe in Jesus are excluded from the family.[16] Critically, by the end of the first century, there are fewer and fewer Jews in the church, and by the end of the second century, Christians begin to outnumber Jews in the empire. These factors combine to produce a situation in which the church's use of the metaphor of Israel becomes more deeply problematic than ever.

Although none of these New Testament writers could possibly have envisioned what was to be done with their words in later Christian history, a great deal of wickedness has been wrought with the metaphor of the church as Israel. Already in the second and third centuries, the Epistle of Barnabas, the writings of Marcion of Sinope, the letters of Ignatius of Antioch, and Melito of Sardis's *Paschal Homily* argue that Christianity has superseded Judaism as the only proper way to honor the God of Israel. Growing Christian majorities begin to marginalize their Jewish neighbors, not only religiously but also socially. By the fourth century, Christians have become sufficiently numerous as to capture the loyalty of the Emperor Constantine. New Testament texts that originally seek to make sense of the emerging church's relationship with the synagogue and its own heritage in the Jewish scriptures become weapons in the hands of powerful Christians against powerless Jews. Centuries of violent pogroms against Jewish ghettos in Europe are fueled by cries of "You are from your father the devil." (John 8:44 NRSV).

Melito, writing in the late second century, holds the dubious distinction of being the first Christian to accuse the Jews of deicide (the murder of God), largely on the basis of Matthew 27:25: "Let his blood be on us and on our children." Matthew very likely intends that sentence to be ironic, to say both that the Jewish authorities who persuade Pilate to convict Jesus and the crowd that calls for his death are culpable, and also that Jesus' saving blood is indeed—at least potentially—on them and their descendants. In the hands of Melito and many of his theological descendants, the Bible verse becomes instead a call to arms, and countless Jews are victimized by Christians as a result.

There is a chilling scene in Claude Lanzmann's 1985 film about the Holocaust, *Shoah*, in which Lanzmann interviews some elderly citizens of Chełmno, Poland, about their memories of the events that transpired there in 1941.[17] Some 152,000 Jewish men, women, and children were rounded up, fifty or so at a time, and imprisoned in a church before being loaded into trucks retrofitted to send the exhaust fumes into the backs of the trucks to kill the people by carbon monoxide poisoning. The people Lanzmann interviews in front of that same church decades later all remember what happened, they say. Lanzmann asks his translator to ask, "Why do they think all this happened to the Jews?" and one man, a Mr. Kantarowski, tells a story that he has heard from a friend about what happened in Myndjewyce, near Warsaw.

> The Jews were gathered in a square. The rabbi asked an SS man: "Can I talk to them?" The SS man said yes. So the rabbi said that around two thousand years ago the Jews condemned the innocent Christ to death. And when they did that, they cried out: "Let his blood fall on our heads and on our sons' heads." Then the rabbi told them: "Perhaps the time has come for that, so let us do nothing, let us go, let us do as we're asked."

26

"He thinks the Jews expiated the death of Christ?" asks Lanzmann. "He doesn't think so, or even that Christ sought revenge. He didn't say that. The rabbi said it. It was God's will, that's all!"[18]

There is no way a Polish rabbi would have said any such thing, quoting Christian scripture as he and his people are about to be murdered by the Nazis, but forty years after the fact a man from Chełmno *thinks* he remembers the story because he has heard Matthew 27:25 interpreted this way so many times himself. This is how scripture can function in Christian imagination when there is no counternarrative, no alternative interpretation that refuses to demonize Jews who do not believe in Jesus.

The historian and political scientist Raul Hilberg suggests that there have been three basic anti-Jewish policies in Western culture, each one arising from the one before it: conversion, expulsion, and annihilation. After Christians become the majority of the Empire in the fourth century, they continue to evangelize their Jewish neighbors as they have from the beginning. Their efforts largely fail, however, so by the sixteenth century some of their magistrates exclude unconverted Jews into walled-off communities within cities called ghettoes.[19] Hilberg chronicles the way the German Nazis use historic rationales and practices to justify anti-Semitism until finally they create "the final solution."

> The missionaries of Christianity had said in effect: You have no right to live among us as Jews. The secular rulers who followed had proclaimed: You have no right to live among us. The German Nazis at last decreed: You have no right to live.[20]

This is what can happen when a metaphor dies, that is, when it becomes literalized and absolutized, and thus loses its life-giving, imaginative power: it ceases to function as a metaphor and becomes instead an instrument of death. When the church thinks of itself as the "new Israel" or "true Israel," it has stopped thinking metaphorically and instead appropriated Israel's identity for itself. That cannot help but become violent, even if the first uses of the metaphor were in the service of defining the church's identity and mission and interpreting God's saving intentions for the world.

The metaphor arises in the ministry of Jesus as a call to join God in the work of redemption, restoring the covenant God extends to the

27

whole world through Israel. When it no longer functions as a metaphor and instead becomes an absolute claim of identity against other claims, it becomes violent. In the years since the Holocaust, the Roman Catholic Church and numerous Protestant denominations have begun to repudiate the "teaching of contempt" that characterized Christian attitudes toward Jews for so long.

> When [Pope John Paul II] made his pilgrimage to the Western Wall [in Jerusalem] in March 2000, the media focused on the apology for anti-Semitism contained in the note he placed between the stones. But the real story was the wording of that message: the pope referred to the Jews as "the people of the covenant," repudiating 2,000 years of supersessionism, Christianity's insistence that the blessings of the covenant were no longer valid for the "old Israel" and had been usurped by the Church.[21]

The danger is not inherent in the metaphor itself, but in its use—or abuse. When a metaphor substitutes for that to which it points, it becomes an idol. Carl Jung warned nearly a century ago of the dangers of idolatry that attend religious literalism. "In Jung's estimation biblical literalism was the accidental offspring of the Protestant Reformation which in time, and in certain quarters, sought to countermand papal authority with an inerrant theology of its own, namely scripture, and with indisputable claims on its true meaning."[22]

Finally, Willie James Jennings traces what is perhaps the most insidious and wicked outgrowth of the church's doctrine of supercessionism, the theological roots of the concept of race and the development of white supremacy.[23] Beginning in the fifteenth century with the inauguration of the European slave trade, Christian thinkers over the next several hundred years find theological ways to justify their absolute power over black bodies by reflecting on their otherness from white bodies. The categories they use derive directly from the already existing convictions about supercessionism. If God has demonstrated the superiority of Christians over Jews by transferring loyalty from Israel to the church, then God has similarly demonstrated the superiority of white Christians over the people of color they enslave and colonize.

Theologian Hans Küng argues that the power of the image of the church as the people of God, which is at the heart of the metaphor of Israel, is that it emphasizes movement rather than stasis, growth rather than institutionalization.[24] In this he is more influenced by Paul than by other New Testament writers, because Paul too sees the church as a movement rather than as an institution, the beachhead of the advancing realm of God that is even now redeeming the world God loves, the world for which Christ died. Paul alone of New Testament writers refuses to allow the church to appropriate Israel's identity because for him what is at stake is theology—the character of God—rather than Christology—the person of Christ. His argument in Romans 9–11 preserves the integrity of God's faithfulness to Israel because, unless God remains faithful to Israel, God cannot be trusted to remain faithful to the church. It is his affirmation in 8:38-39 that elicits what follows:

> I am convinced that neither death, nor life, nor angels, nor rulers, nor things present, nor things to come, nor powers, nor height, nor depth, nor anything else in all creation, will be able to separate us [and, by implication, Israel] from the love of God in Christ Jesus our Lord. (NRSV)

For Further Reading

Ruether, Rosemary Radford. *Faith and Fratricide: The Theological Roots of Anti-Semitism*. New York: Seabury, 1979.

Siker, Jeffrey S. *Disinheriting the Jews: Abraham in Early Christian Controversy*. Louisville, KY: Westminster John Knox, 1991.

Chapter 3

God's House and Priesthood: The Church as Temple

The temple is the most explicitly cultic metaphor for the church in the New Testament since, by definition, the temple belongs to God. The other metaphors explored here—Israel, the body of Christ, family, and agricultural images—derive from more human contexts, even though they take on elevated meanings when applied to the church. The temple is holy from the beginning, though, because it is God's house.

God's holiness and the people's obligation to recognize that holiness through adoration, prayer, and sacrifice mark Israel's worship from the very beginning. After the flood, before there even is Israel, Noah builds an altar to the Lord (Gen 8:20). So does Abram when God promises him land and offspring (12:7). Later, Abraham builds an altar on Mount Moriah where God instructs him to sacrifice his son Isaac and then provides instead a ram for the offering (22:1-19). After the Exodus from Egypt, there are portable altars that accompany the people on their journeys, designed by God (Exod 17:15; 20:24-26; 27:1; etc.). Israel's God steadfastly resists being seen by mortals despite being repeatedly revealed—in a burning bush (Exod 3:2), in a pillar of fire and the smoke that comes from the fire (13:21), in the sound of sheer silence (1 Kgs 19:12), and so on. God becomes most accessible, even though invisible, in worship. Michael Hundley observes,

> In a dangerous and volatile world, the ancient Near Eastern temple was the primary point of intersection between human and divine. As a principal means of establishing security in an otherwise insecure world, it situated the deity in the midst of human habitation, so that humanity might offer service and gifts in exchange for divine protection and prosperity.[1]

How different that is from what most postmodern Western people experience. Pulitzer Prize-winning author Annie Dillard observes of much contemporary Christian (mostly Protestant) worship,

> Why do people in church seem like cheerful, brainless tourists on a packaged tour of the Absolute?...Does anyone have the foggiest idea what sort of power we blithely invoke? Or, as I suspect, does no one believe a word of it? The churches are children playing on the floor with their chemistry sets, mixing up a batch of TNT to kill a Sunday morning. It is madness to wear ladies' straw hats and velvet hats to church; we should all be wearing crash helmets. Ushers should issue life preservers and signal flares; they should lash us to our pews. For the sleeping god may wake someday and take offense, or the waking god may draw us to where we can never return.[2]

Israel's Temple(s)

The Old Testament speaks repeatedly of the temple in Jerusalem as God's house, the place Israel can reliably expect to encounter God. Brennan Breed compares the temple to a nuclear reactor, an immeasurably powerful force that is at once awesome and full of potential danger to human beings.[3] Throughout Leviticus, God instructs the priests repeatedly to put the blood of sacrificed animals on all sides of the altar (1:5, 11, 15; 3:2; etc.). Blood makes the altar holy because blood is holiness itself.[4] This is why Israel is forbidden to consume blood (Gen 9:4; Lev 7:26-27; 17:10-14; 19:26, etc.).

Before there is a temple there is a tabernacle, a portable tent rather than a fixed edifice. God summons Moses, Aaron, Aaron's sons Nadab and Abihu, and seventy elders of Israel to Mount Sinai and reveals to them there the appropriate worship of the God who has just made a covenant with them (Exod 24:1-11). God then prescribes in intricate detail the creation of the tabernacle, its furnishings, most importantly the ark of God, and the priesthood that will lead Israel in its worship (24:12–31:18). Tabernacle worship is not a human creation—what we might call "religion"—but is designed by God for God's own habitation. It is suffused with the very holiness of God.

Holiness is sometimes a difficult concept for twenty-first-century people to come to terms with because it conjures up visions of self-righteous people we accuse of being "holier than thou." It carries a connotation of moralism. The Bible, though, talks about holiness not as a characteristic of people but a characteristic—or better, the defining characteristic—of God. People and places and things become holy by God's action, and they must be holy if they are to be in the presence of God. William Brown says Israel's temple is conceived to be a microcosm of creation, heaven and earth come together as God intended. Creation is itself the first temple, the place God speaks into being (Gen 1:2) and then walks through (3:8). All other humanly constructed temples are microcosms of the original.[5] "In Israelite, Jewish, and early Christian imagination the terms 'creation,' 'heaven and earth,' and 'temple' function homologically," that is, they are sufficiently alike in meaning that they can stand in for one another, notes Stanley Saunders, which is to say that, although there is a building identified as God's temple, we do well to remember that all of creation is intended to be God's temple.[6] "The Temple is an *eikōn*, an image, an epitome of the world."[7]

Holiness is the very nature of God, who is frequently called "the Holy One" (1 Kgs 19:22; Isa 1:4; 5:19; Ps 89:19). Holiness is the quality that sets God apart from the world even as God acts and moves in the world, and whatever God touches becomes holy as a consequence. At Bethel (the name means "house of God"), Jacob sees a vision of God's angels ascending and descending a ladder from heaven and he declares the place sacred, because it is a window into the fact that heaven and earth are really together and only God can cross their boundaries (Gen 28:11-22). When God comes to

Moses in the burning bush, Moses must remove his shoes because he is in the presence of holiness (Exod 3:5). The angels who sing "Holy, holy, holy" around God's throne burn Isaiah's lips with coals to purify his mouth and enable him to say what God tells him to say (Isa 6:3, 7).[8]

The tabernacle contains the ark, a box "forty-five inches long, twenty-seven inches wide, and twenty-seven inches high" (Exod 25:10). It contains at first the Urim and Thummim, dice used by the high priest to determine the answers to yes-and-no questions addressed to God (Num 27:21; 1 Sam 14:41; 28:6), some of the ways they learned the desires of God for the community.[9] Subsequently it holds the tablets of the law of Moses, which is why it is also frequently called the ark of the covenant. The ark is suspended between poles used to carry it around and is full of so much holy power that to touch it—even accidentally—is to die (Num 4:15; compare 2 Sam 6:1-7; 1 Chron 13:9-12). This is because the ark is identified so closely with the presence of God that its holiness is all-consuming. In Num 10:35-36, Moses addresses the ark as if he is speaking to God.

> Whenever the ark set out, Moses would say,
> "Arise, O Lord, let your enemies be scattered,
>   and your foes flee before you."
> And whenever it came to rest, he would say,
>   "Return, O Lord of the ten thousand thousands of Israel."
>   (NRSV)[10]

The tabernacle continues to function, being carried around as needed—including into battle—until Solomon consolidates power in Jerusalem, some three hundred years later, and builds the temple (1 Kgs 6–8; 2 Chron 2–4). In 1 Kings 8:4-7 the ark moves into the temple, which then takes on all the same characteristics as the tabernacle.[11]

After King David defeats his enemies, he decides to build God a house as fine as his own. "See now, I am living in a house of cedar, but the ark of God stays in a tent" (2 Sam 7:2 NRSV). God responds, though, "Are you the one to build me a house to live in? I have not lived in a house since the day I brought up the people of Israel from Egypt to this day, but

I have been moving about in a tent and a tabernacle" (vv. 5b-6). Instead God promises to build David a house rather than letting David build one for God. The house God intends, though, is not a building but a family, a dynasty that will last forever (vv. 11b-16). It will remain to David's son to build God a house.

> Solomon sent the following message to Hiram: "You know that my father David wasn't able to build a temple for the name of the Lord my God. This was because of the enemies that fought him on all sides until the Lord put them under the soles of his feet. Now the Lord my God has given me peace on every side, without enemies or misfortune. So I'm planning to build a temple for the name of the Lord my God, just as the Lord indicated to my father David, 'I will give you a son to follow you on your throne. He will build the temple for my name.'" (1 Kgs 5:2-5; compare 2 Sam 7:13)

The completed temple is indeed a place Israel can expect to encounter God, as the story of Samuel in 1 Samuel 3:1-18 so vividly demonstrates. It is also the source of the people's confidence in God's providential care. Isaiah says,

> When the lion growls,
> the young lion, over its prey,
>   though a band of shepherds is summoned against it,
>   isn't scared off by their noise
>   or frightened by their roar.
> So the Lord of heavenly forces will go down
>   to fight on Mount Zion [where the temple stands] and on her hill.
> Like birds flying aloft,
>   so the Lord of heavenly forces will shield Jerusalem:
>   shielding and saving, sparing and rescuing. (Isa 31:4-5)

Rather than a space for people to come together, as we think of synagogues and as Protestant churches describe themselves, the temple is God's house, and priests make offerings on the nation's behalf, although they often assemble in the outer court as the whole people of God.[12] Roman Catholic and Orthodox churches retain much of Israel's sense of God's house.

As the nation's political fortunes wane in the sixth century BCE, and the neo-Babylonian empire threatens to invade, court prophets repeat Isaiah of Jerusalem's promises. Jeremiah makes fun of their assuring the people that the temple's presence will protect them from their enemies, though. He brands their slogan instead a deception (7:4), and urges them to prepare for disaster. Jeremiah, of course, is sadly correct. Solomon's temple is destroyed in 587 BCE, although the people who are not deported to Babylon continue to gather on its foundation to offer sacrifices (2 Kgs 25:8-17). The exilic prophet Haggai traces the misfortunes of the people—famine, drought, and so on—to their failure to rebuild God's house. "Is it time for you to dwell in your own paneled houses while this house [the temple] lies in ruins?" (1:4).

The temple Jesus and the first Christians know is the second one constructed, supported by a grant from the Persian king Cyrus (Ezra 3:7-13), and built after the exile between 520 and 515 BCE. It is later vastly expanded by Herod the Great (reigned 37 BCE–4 CE) as a way to impress the Romans, on whose behalf he rules, about the importance of the Jewish kingdom and of himself as their vassal.[13] It is a huge complex with multiple courtyards and inner rooms, all surrounding the holy of holies, where only the high priest enters and only once a year on the Day of Atonement. The temple complex is not only the central physical feature of Jerusalem, sitting as it does on a hill; it is also the dominant social reality as well. During the monarchy, it legitimizes the king; under imperial occupation, authority shifts to the priesthood and the temple embodies the collaboration between the landed aristocracy and their Roman overlords. In a very real sense, the first-century temple functions something like the National Bank of Israel, where commerce and politics are nearly as important as religion.[14]

Jesus and the Second Temple

The physical temple figures prominently in Luke–Acts, as both the Gospel (1:5-23; 24:53) and Acts (2:46; 26:21) begin and end with references to it, and Luke alone tells the story of the boy Jesus in the temple, astounding his elders with his precocious understanding of scripture (Luke

36

2:22-34).[15] It is Mark, however, who makes the greatest metaphorical use of the temple.

After Jesus enters Jerusalem in the week leading up to the Passover at the end of his ministry (Mark 11:1-10), the evangelist makes a seemingly banal observation: "Jesus entered Jerusalem and went into the temple. After he looked around at everything, because it was already late in the evening, he returned to Bethany with the Twelve" (11:11). It sounds almost as though Jesus is a tourist. What the small paragraph does, however, is set up a literary intercalation, the sandwiching of two stories that mutually interpret each other.[16]

The next paragraph, verses 12-14, is even stranger than verse 11. On his way back to the capital city from Bethany, Jesus sees a fig tree and curses it never to bear fruit again, despite the fact that it is not "the season for figs" (v. 13). Mark says Jesus is hungry, but it seems silly, even petulant for him to be angry at the tree when it is not the season for figs.

Then we return to Jerusalem where Jesus curses the temple because it has become, in the words of Jeremiah, "a hiding place for criminals" (Jer 7:11) rather than—quoting Isaiah—"a house of prayer for all nations" (Isa 56:7; Mark 11:16). Although Christian tradition calls this story the "cleansing" of the temple, it is difficult to see how Jesus makes it any cleaner by turning over the tables of those who sell sacrificial animals and those who convert foreign currency (especially coins that bear the emperor's image) into local money that is permitted in God's house. This is where the fig tree episode and the temple incident interpret each other. It is not the season for figs (and we do well here to remember who is in charge of the seasons), and apparently it is not the season for the temple, either. Mark says God intends it to be for all nations, not just for Israel, but it has instead become "a hideout for crooks" (11:17), which is Jeremiah's earlier indictment of the leaders of Judah who wrongly think the presence of God's house will save them from the inevitable invasion of the Babylonian army.

> Jesus' charge against the temple authorities coheres with his charge against the Pharisees and scribes. In each case, humans have usurped or eclipsed the intention of God by setting up boundaries that work contrary to God's intention for creation.... The Pharisees' system of

holiness and the worship and rites practiced in the temple were designed to safeguard God's presence among Israel. They have, however, had the opposite effect: They have erected boundaries to keep God at a safe distance and to restrict access to God.[17]

The word translated "crooks" is better rendered "bandits" or "terrorists," because it refers not generally to people who deal dishonestly but specifically to revolutionary fighters who hold people up on the highway to support their guerilla war efforts against Rome. The man helped by the good Samaritan in Luke 10:30-37 is attacked by such bandits, for example (v. 30). The same word occurs twice more in Mark, at 14:48, where Jesus asks those who arrest him, "Have you come out with swords and clubs to arrest me as though I were a bandit?" (NRSV), and at 15:27, where the two men crucified with Jesus are identified as bandits.[18] The temple has ceased to operate as a house of prayer for all nations, and Jesus curses it just as he curses the fig tree. Jesus' actions in the temple constitute a prophetic sign-action, much like those of the biblical prophets,[19] a "dramatic demonstration meant to predict the imminent destruction of the temple."[20]

The following paragraph begins with Peter's amazement the next morning as Jesus and the Twelve again pass by the fig tree. "Rabbi, look how the fig tree you cursed has dried up" (11:21). This confirms for the reader that Jesus' prophetic words have power. Just as the fig tree has withered, so will the temple, we are meant to conclude. Then Jesus offers a little homily on the nature of true worship.

> Have faith in God! I assure you that whoever says to this mountain, "Be lifted up and thrown into the sea"—and doesn't waver but believes that what is said will really happen—it will happen. Therefore I say to you, whatever you pray and ask for, believe that you will receive it, and it will be so for you. And whenever you stand up to pray, if you have something against anyone, forgive so that your Father in heaven may forgive you your wrongdoings. (11:22-25)

The proper worship of God, he says, consists of faith, prayer, and forgiveness rather than sacrificial offerings. The community of the church that has faith in Jesus, prays, and forgives as it is forgiven will replace the temple cult as the proper worship of the God of Israel.²¹ Later, in 12:28-34, a scribe, an expert in the law of God, asks Jesus what is the greatest commandment and Jesus responds by saying there are two: love of God (Deut 6:4-5) and love of neighbor (Lev 19:18). The scribe approves of Jesus' answer, repeats it back to him, and then adds something Jesus has not said, that love of God and neighbor are "much more important than all kinds of entirely burned offerings and sacrifices" (Mark 12:33). Jesus then praises him and says, "You aren't far from God's kingdom" (v. 34). Evidently, the scribe understands what the fig tree and temple story mean.

What Jesus does implicitly by turning over tables in the temple he talks about explicitly in chapter 13. "As Jesus left the temple, one of his disciples said to him, 'Teacher, look! What awesome stones and buildings!' Jesus responded, 'Do you see these enormous buildings? Not even one stone will be left upon another. All will be demolished'" (13:1-2). He then proceeds to detail the eschatological conditions that are about to overtake the world as God brings about the promised redemption: cosmic and social turmoil, hostility toward Jesus' friends and followers, desecration of the temple, and the coming of the Son of Man on the clouds to gather his elect. Jesus' sermon about the last days ends with a parable about a householder who leaves town entrusting his staff with the work of maintaining the house in his absence, not a bad image for the church that awaits Jesus' return from heaven, where he sits at God's right hand, subjecting God's enemies (12:36; 14:62).

The picture of Jesus at God's right hand is taken from Psalm 110:1, which originally addressed the king:

> The LORD says to my lord,
> "Sit at my right hand
> until I make your enemies your footstool." (NRSV)

This Bible verse is the single most frequently quoted or alluded to in the entire New Testament.²² It helps early Christians explain where Jesus is and what he is doing following his resurrection and ascension and what they can anticipate at his coming in glory. Sitting at God's right hand,

Jesus has the place of highest honor in God's court, and he helps God subdue the enemies that defy God's saving purpose in the world.[23]

At Jesus' trial before the Sanhedrin, Mark has the council violate a number of biblical requirements for proper legal procedure. They go out looking for testimony against Jesus (14:55), although they find none. They accept testimony from lying witnesses (compare Exod 20:16; 23:1; Deut 5:20), and the witnesses do not agree with each other. Deuteronomy 19:15-20 says such conflicting testimony should be thrown out. The lying witnesses who do not agree with each other nevertheless make a very precise accusation against Jesus: "We heard him saying, 'I will destroy this temple, constructed by humans, and within three days I will build another, one not made by humans'" (Mark 14:58). Mark has not attributed those words to Jesus before this moment, but the astute listener will remember Jesus' cursing the fig tree and the temple, the scribe's words in chapter 12, and Jesus' prediction in chapter 13 and recognize that the lying witnesses have ironically told the unvarnished truth: the Christian community about to come into being will replace the Jerusalem temple that is about to be destroyed.

> [In 11:12-25] Mark has crafted a story that depicts the community of Jesus' followers performing the function of the eschatological temple of God. That community is the house of prayer for all peoples, the place of eschatological in-gathering that endures after God's judgment comes upon the bandits' den that is the Jerusalem temple.[24]

Even before the Romans destroy the physical temple in Jerusalem—and there is good reason to think Mark's book is composed during the revolt rather than after it[25]—Christians like Mark believe that their communities perform the functions of God's temple as they engage in faith, prayer, and forgiveness.

Finally, when Jesus dies, as darkness covers the land, "The curtain of the sanctuary [is] torn in two from top to bottom" and the centurion at the cross makes the only unsilenced confession of Jesus' identity in Mark's book: "This man was certainly God's son" (15:38-39). The image of the curtain's being ripped echoes the picture in 1:10 of the heavens being ripped open (the same word is used both places), and the specification that the ripping is "from top to bottom" says God is the implied actor. "The image may suggest that the protecting barriers are gone," says Donald Juel, "and that God, unwilling to be confined to sacred spaces, is on the loose in our realm."[26]

The word translated "not made by humans" in Mark 14:58 is literally "not made with hands," and it recurs at 2 Corinthians 5:1, where Paul says, "We know that if the tent that we live in on earth is torn down, we have a building from God. It's a house that isn't handmade, which is eternal and located in heaven." The subject there seems to be Christians' individual bodies as Paul contemplates their mortality but points also to their life together as a tent—a tabernacle—and the coincidence of houses "made with hands" and houses "not made with hands" is striking. Even more striking is Hebrews 9:11, where we find a contrast between a physical temple and a spiritual one. "But Christ has appeared as the high priest of the good things that have happened. He passed through the greater and more perfect meeting tent [or tabernacle], which isn't made by human hands (that is, it's not a part of this world)."[27] John's Jesus says something remarkably similar to the Samaritan woman at the well:

> Believe me, woman, the time is coming when you and your people will worship the Father neither on this mountain [that is, Mount Gerizim, where Samaritans worship] nor in Jerusalem. You and your people worship what you don't know; we worship what we know because salvation is from the Jews. But the time is coming—and is here!—when true worshippers will worship in spirit and truth. The Father looks for those who worship him this way. (John 4:21-23)[28]

Paul

"The prescripts to the Pauline letters name the members of the churches as *hagioi* ['holy ones' or 'saints'],"[29] notes Georg Strecker. "Christians are thus designated with the same term used in the Old Testament to describe priests."[30] At 1 Corinthians 3:10-17, in the context of explaining how the Corinthians ought to understand his and Apollos's respective work among them, Paul says,

I laid a foundation like a wise master builder according to God's grace that was given to me, but someone else [Apollos] is building on top of it. Each person needs to pay attention to the way they build on it. No one can lay any other foundation besides the one that is already laid, which is Jesus Christ. So, whether someone builds on top of the foundation with gold, silver, precious stones, wood, grass, or hay, each one's work will be clearly shown. The day will make it clear, because it will be revealed with fire—the fire will test the quality of each one's work. If anyone's work survives, they'll get a reward. But if anyone's work goes up in flames, they'll lose it. However, they themselves will be saved as if they had gone through a fire. Don't you know that you [plural] are God's temple and God's Spirit lives in you? If someone destroys God's temple, God will destroy that person, because God's temple is holy, which is what you are.[31]

Paul's work of establishing the church in Corinth lays the foundation for Apollos's subsequent labor among the people as preacher and teacher. What the two men accomplish is the creation of a worshipping community that either survives God's judgment—if it is made with gold, silver, precious stones—or does not—if it is wood, grass, or hay. Temples, says Jill Marshall, "maintain holiness by being off limits to certain people and by requiring purification rituals...and most important, a temple is the dwelling place of a god."[32] The apostolic mission builds a temple for God to live in, even though it is composed of human beings rather than stones.

At 1 Corinthians 6:19 Paul says something very similar: "Or don't you know that your [plural] body [singular] is a temple of the Holy Spirit who is in you? Don't you know that you have the Holy Spirit from God, and you don't belong to yourselves?" The "body" he mentions here refers both to the physical bodies of individual believers and to the gathered body that is the church.[33] Both individually and as a community, Christians are to live such holy lives that God will dwell among them. Again, at 2 Corinthians 6:16 he says,

What agreement has the temple of God with idols? For we are the temple of the living God; as God said,

> "I will live in them and walk among them,
> and I will be their God,
> and they shall be my people [Lev 26:11-12]." (NRSV)

At Rom 12:1-2 he further specifies the priestly function the church serves.

> So, brothers and sisters, because of God's mercies, I encourage you to present your bodies as a living sacrifice that is holy and pleasing to God. This is your appropriate priestly service. Don't be conformed to the patterns of this world, but be transformed by the renewing of your minds so that you can figure out what God's will is—what is good and pleasing and mature.

Ephesians

The writer of Ephesians describes his addressees as a building that is not specifically called a temple but is likely intended to be. "As God's household [the word means 'house' as well as 'family'], you are built on the foundation of the apostles and prophets with Christ Jesus himself as the cornerstone" (2:20). The word "foundation" recalls Paul's similar usage in 1 Corinthians 3, particularly with the modifier "apostles and prophets." Ephesians advances Paul's building metaphor from 1 Corinthians 3: no longer is Christ the foundation; the apostles and prophets are, and Christ is the cornerstone.[34]

The picture is further developed here with the description of Christ as "cornerstone." Just as Psalm 110:1 helps early Christians make sense of Christ's postresurrection work, so two other Bible verses repeatedly help them interpret his rejection by the religious authorities and his exaltation by God. The Psalmist says, "The stone that the builders rejected has become the chief cornerstone" (118:22 NRSV) and Isaiah says,

> Therefore thus says the Lord God,
> See, I am laying in Zion a foundation stone,
>   a tested stone,
> a precious cornerstone, a sure foundation:
>   "One who trusts will not panic." (28:16 NRSV)

Together, these two verses function for Christians to describe Jesus as both rejected by human powers and exalted by God. They further describe him as the most basic element of the human building that is the church. The cornerstone of a building is the first stone laid and the one to which all the others are aligned. Christ is God's initiation of the Christian community, and its members are all connected to him.[35]

First Peter

The letter called 1 Peter extends the image and says the church is both the temple and its priesthood. Furthermore, just as Christ was rejected by human beings and vindicated by God, so are his followers.

> Now you are coming to [Christ] as to a living stone. Even though this stone was rejected by humans, from God's perspective it is chosen, valuable. You yourselves are being built like living stones into a spiritual temple. You are being made into a holy priesthood to offer up spiritual sacrifices that are acceptable to God through Jesus Christ. Thus it is written in scripture, *Look! I am laying a cornerstone in Zion, chosen, valuable. The person who believes in him will never be shamed.* So God honors you who believe. For those who refuse to believe, though, the stone the builders tossed aside has become the capstone [or cornerstone]. This is a stone that makes people stumble and a rock that makes them fall. Because they refuse to believe in the word, they stumble. Indeed, this is the end to which they were appointed. But you are a chosen race, a royal priesthood, a holy nation, a people who are God's own possession. You have become this people so that you may speak of the wonderful acts of the one who called you out of darkness into his amazing light. Once you weren't a people, but now you are God's people. Once you hadn't received mercy, but now you have received mercy. (2:4-10)

A similar knitting together of Bible verses about stones occurs at Romans 9:33, with Isaiah 28:16 and 8:14 together serving to describe Christian preaching of the gospel rather than the person of Christ. "See, I am putting in Zion a stone of stumbling and a rock of scandal, and the one who trusts in it will not be put to shame."[36] The "shame" here is not personal embarrassment but eschatological collapse. That is, Paul says the good news of God's impartiality and faithfulness to Jews and Gentiles alike can be trusted to sustain Christians at the last judgment.

Hebrews

In Hebrews, Christ is the high priest of God's temple, the church:

> Therefore, brothers and sisters who are partners in the heavenly calling, think about Jesus, the apostle and high priest of our confession. Jesus was faithful to the one who appointed him just like Moses was faithful in God's house. But he deserves greater glory than Moses in the same way that the builder of the house deserves more honor than the house itself. Every house is built by someone, but God is the builder of everything. (3:1-4)

Although the figure of Melchizedek appears in the Bible only at Genesis 14:18, he plays a prominent role in Hebrews (5:6-10; 6:20; 7:1-17). This is because of another verse from Psalm 110 that assures the king of victory over his enemies: "The LORD has sworn and will not change his mind, 'You are a priest forever according to the order of Melchizedek'" (110:4 NRSV). In Genesis 14, Melchizedek, a Canaanite priest-king who appears out of nowhere and disappears just as quickly, blesses both Abram and Abram's God and receives a payment of tribute from Abram in return. How he comes to be thought of as a priest and eventually as a semidivine figure is not all that clear, but in addition to Hebrews, he shows up also in 2 Enoch, a Second Temple Jewish book, and texts from Qumran.[37] The writer of Hebrews quotes Psalm 110:4 to explain the superior character of Jesus' priesthood: it is both ancient and eternal.

Christ is not only God's high priest in Hebrews, his death is also the sacrifice he offers to God on the church's behalf. Christ's sacrifice is ultimate because it is willing; although a son he learned obedience (5:7-9). He is furthermore not only an atoning sacrifice but also a model for Christians to emulate. This argument seems to address the universal conviction in antiquity that religions must have physical temples and offerings. Christianity does not have one, which might make it look inferior to other religions. Hebrews responds that not only does Christianity have a cult, it has the best one because it is spiritual rather than physical.

John

In John's Gospel, the story in which Jesus turns over tables in the temple is clearly the same incident as in Matthew, Mark, and Luke, although it is interpreted very differently. To begin with, John moves the story from the end of Jesus' ministry to the beginning, and it does not provoke Jesus' arrest, as it does in the Synoptics.[38] Rather, it sets the agenda for the first half of John's book: Jesus himself replaces not only the temple but all major Jewish festivals.

> It was nearly time for the Jewish Passover, and Jesus went up to Jerusalem. He found in the temple those who were selling cattle, sheep, and doves, as well as those involved in exchanging currency sitting there. He made a whip from ropes and chased them all out of the temple, including the cattle and the sheep. He scattered the coins and overturned the tables of those who exchanged currency. He said to the dove sellers, "Get these things out of here! Don't make my Father's house a place of business." His disciples remembered that it is written, *Passion for your house consumes me.* Then the Jewish leaders asked him, "By what authority are you doing these things? What miraculous sign will you show us?" Jesus answered, "Destroy this temple and in three days I'll raise it up." The Jewish leaders replied, "It took forty-six years to build this temple, and you will raise it up in three days?" But the temple Jesus was talking about was his body. After he was raised from the dead, his disciples remembered what he had said, and they believed the scripture and the word that Jesus had spoken. (John 2:13-22)

In John the church does not replace the temple; Jesus does.[39]

Revelation

Finally, John of Patmos describes the church as the pillars of the temple: "As for those who emerge victorious, I will make them pillars in the temple of my God, and they will never leave it. I will write on them the name of my God and the name of the city of my God, the New Jerusalem that comes down out of heaven from my God" (Rev 3:12). The seer has repeated visions that take place in God's heavenly temple (7:15; 11:1-2, 19; 14:15, 17; 15:5–16:1; 16:17) and his final vision concerns the reuniting of heaven and earth, the establishment of the New Jerusalem in which there is no temple "because its temple is the LORD God Almighty and the Lamb" (21:22).[40]

Incense

Occasionally in the New Testament the image for the church is not of the temple generally but one of its activities, specifically the burning of incense. Burning certain ingredients together, usually on hot coals, to produce aromatic smoke (the word *incense* comes from the Latin word for "burn") was a widespread practice throughout the Ancient Near East, and the Israelites offered incense to God both in the tabernacle and in the temple.[41] "Aaron will burn sweet-smelling incense on the incense altar every morning when he takes care of the lamps. And again when Aaron lights the lamps at twilight, he will burn incense. It should be a regular incense offering in the LORD's presence in every generation" (Exod 30:7-8). The vision of sweet-smelling smoke wafting up toward heaven seems to carry with it the prayers of Israel. It also recalls Exodus 13:21 with the pillar of fire that signifies God's accompaniment of the people through the wilderness and Exodus 19:18 with the smoke that enshrouds Mount Sinai as God descends on it in fire. The Psalmist says, "Let my prayer stand before you like incense" (141:2).

So also New Testament writers employ the metaphor of incense to talk about their ministries. In 2 Corinthians, Paul compares the church's proclamation of the gospel rather than its prayers to incense.

> But thank God, who is always leading us around through Christ as if we were in a parade. He releases the fragrance of the knowledge of him everywhere through us. We [Christian preachers] smell like the aroma of Christ's offering to God, both to those who are being saved and to those who are on the road to destruction. We smell like a contagious dead person to those who are dying, but we smell like the fountain of life to those who are being saved. (2:14-16a)

John of Patmos says that when Jesus, described as a lamb that has been slain and raised from death, is found worthy to open a divine scroll that contains the revelation of what is to happen both in heaven and on earth, "the four living creatures and the twenty-four elders fell down before the Lamb. Each held a harp and gold bowls full of incense, which are the prayers of the saints" (Rev 5:8). The final vision of Revelation portrays the new Jerusalem, the restored heaven and earth that is so completely as God intends it that there is no need for a constructed temple because God's unmediated presence is itself the temple (21:22). The concluding pages of the New Testament show the church, indeed the entire creation, in worship of God. The biblical story of creation is reprised and its intentions restored as "the river of life-giving water" (22:1) recalls Genesis 2:10 where a river flows out of Eden; "the tree of life" (22:2) whose leaves are "for the healing of the nations" recalls the tree of life in Genesis 2:9; "There will no longer be any curse" (22:3), promises the seer, putting to an end God's curse of both the serpent and the first humans (Gen 3:14, 17). "Night will be no more. They won't need the light of a lamp or the light of the sun, for the LORD God will shine on them" (Rev 22:5), which recalls God's first creation of light (Gen 1:3). "The throne of God and the Lamb will be in [the New Jerusalem], and his servants will worship him" (Rev 22:3).

The power of the temple image is its capacity to describe the boundaries of the church as expansive and capable of universal inclusivity as well as bordered by God's holiness. The vision at the end of Revelation sees the entire creation at worship rather than at war. The temple metaphor is an explicit call to holiness; if the church is to be God's house, it must embody God's holiness, which includes not only God's justice but also God's love. Perhaps the greatest promise of the metaphor of temple for the church is its call to the twenty-first-century church to embrace creation care rather than its sometime retreat into a spiritualized distance from the world. There exists also an inherent risk in the image of the church as temple. Our very suspicion of people who are "holier than thou" is fed by the times the church not only retreats from the world but also looks down contemptuously at it.

The Church's Structures and Orders

Unlike the Jerusalem temple or pagan temples, with which the ancients are all very familiar, this Christian temple has no hereditary priesthood, and unlike the rituals of sacrifice and offering entrusted to other priests, the worship leaders of the earliest Christian communities—if we can use a somewhat anachronistic description—do not perform private rituals.[42] Although today there are numerous church offices—ministers, priests, pastors, deacons, elders, bishops, and so on—and the names of those offices all derive from words in the Bible, the meanings attached to the words are not nearly so clear in the New Testament as they seem in contemporary church contexts.[43]

It is important to remember that the earliest Christian groups have precious little structure compared with what we know of modern churches. The relatively small charismatic gatherings we see in the New Testament seem to be quite informal, as the chaos in 1 Corinthians 14 highlights: "When you meet together, each one has a psalm, a teaching, a revelation, a tongue [that is, ecstatic speech], or an interpretation" (v. 26). Paul's advice is that the people take turns and ensure that ecstatic speech is interpreted so that it edifies more than the person who utters it. "In the case of prophets, let two or three speak and have the rest evaluate what is said," he suggests (v. 29).

Prophets

Prophets are ubiquitous in early Christianity. John the Baptist is widely assumed to be a prophet (Matt 14:5; 21:26; Mark 11:32; Luke 20:6), Jesus calls him "more than a prophet" (Matt 11:9; Luke 7:26), and Luke has his father Zechariah say, "And you, child, will be called the prophet of the Most High; for you will go before the Lord to prepare his ways" (1:76). An alternative view finds voice in the Fourth Gospel, where John emphatically denies being "the prophet," that is, the so-called prophet like Moses spoken of in Deuteronomy 18:15 (cf. Acts 3:22; 7:37), a role that is reserved in John for Jesus alone. Jesus is many things to Christians—Messiah, Lord, Savior, and so on—but he is also a prophet. He refers to himself as a prophet[44] and other people describe him as one.[45] The most numerous references to prophets, though, are to Christians who speak on God's behalf—much as Israel's prophets had—under the inspiration of God's Spirit.

We know some early Christian prophets by name. When Jesus' parents bring him to the temple as an infant, the prophet Anna "began to praise God and to speak about Jesus to everyone who was looking forward to the redemption of Jerusalem" (Luke 2:36-38). Philip the evangelist has four unmarried daughters who have the gift of prophecy (Acts 21:9).

At Acts 15:32, Judas and Silas exhort and encourage the believers as prophets in Antioch. At Acts 11:28 a prophet named Agabus predicts a worldwide famine, and at 21:10-14 he predicts Paul's arrest and imprisonment. The Pastor identifies Timothy as a prophet by saying, "Do not neglect the gift that is in you, which was given to you through prophecy with the laying on of hands by the council of elders" (1 Tim 4:14 NRSV).[46] John of Patmos calls himself a prophet and describes his book as prophecy (Rev 1:3; 19:10; 22:7, 10, 18, 19). The close connection between prophecy and teaching is highlighted in this commissioning scene:

> The church at Antioch included prophets and teachers: Barnabas, Simeon (nicknamed Niger), Lucius from Cyrene, Manaen (a childhood friend of Herod the ruler), and Saul. As they were worshipping the Lord and fasting, the Holy Spirit said, "Appoint Barnabas and Saul to the work I have called them to undertake." After they fasted and prayed, they laid their hands on these two and sent them off. (Acts 13:1-3)

Although this laying on of hands likely does not yet constitute ordination the way the church later would define that rite, it certainly lays the groundwork for it. The Pastor tells Timothy, "Don't neglect the spiritual gift in you that was given through prophecy when the elders laid hands on you" (1 Tim 4:14) and "I'm reminding you to revive God's gift that is in you through the laying on of my hands" (2 Tim 1:6).

Apostles

Apostles are a much smaller group of people and seem to be limited to the first generation of the church. The writer of 2 Peter considers them in the past: "I want you to recall what the holy prophets foretold as well as what the Lord and savior commanded through your apostles" (3:2; cf. Jude 17). Mark 6:30 calls the Twelve "apostles" as does Acts 1:1-2. Paul is very specific about the definition—an apostle is someone appointed by Christ to establish churches—and repeatedly calls himself one (Rom 1:1, 5; 11:13; 1 Cor 1:1; etc.). He includes people like the married couple Andronicus and Junia (Rom 16:7) and Titus (2 Cor 8:23), among others, in the category. Luke operates with a more fluid definition, calling Paul and Barnabas apostles at 14:4, 6, 14, even though they do not meet the criteria he earlier

50

sets up for replacing Judas of having followed Jesus "from the baptism of John until the day when Jesus was taken from us" (1:22). Paul also has to defend his apostleship from criticism from others (2 Cor 11–12; Gal 1:1).

The figures of the prophet and the apostle seem to fade from prominence after the first century, but other functions become more important, particularly elders, deacons, and bishops. No one appoints someone a prophet or deacon in the first generation, although it may be that someone— like an apostle—puts in place bishops or "overseers" in individual communities. Paul seems to think it is God who does the appointing: "In the church, God has appointed first apostles, second prophets, third teachers, then miracles, then gifts of healing, the ability to help others, leadership skills, different kinds of tongues" (1 Cor 12:28; cf. Eph 4:11). Titus 1:5, though, suggests that the authority to put leaders in place is later delegated to human leaders. "The reason I left you behind in Crete was to organize whatever needs to be done and to appoint elders in each city, as I told you."

Elders

Roger Beckwith argues that the function of Christian elders derives from a similar role in the synagogue, where the most senior members exercise authority not simply because of their age but also due to their social status.[47] It may be that early on "elder" was a term of honor in the synagogue rather than a specific office, and the same may be true of the church.[48] It is even likely that the hosts of house churches were considered elders by virtue of their patronage of the congregations. Elders appear throughout Acts as distributors of relief aid (11:30), leaders of communities (14:23; 20:17; 21:18), and arbiters of disputes (15:1-29; 16:4). The Pastor speaks of a "council of elders" (1 Tim 4:14 NRSV), says they exercise authority (5:17), and directs Titus "to appoint elders in each city" (Titus 1:5). James 5:14 says elders pray over the sick and anoint them with oil. First Peter addresses elders directly:

> Like shepherds, tend the flock of God among you. Watch over it. Don't shepherd because you must, but do it voluntarily for God. Don't shepherd greedily, but do it eagerly. Don't shepherd by ruling over those

entrusted to your care, but become examples to the flock. And when the chief shepherd appears, you will receive an unfading crown of glory. In the same way, I urge you who are younger: accept the authority of the elders. (5:2-5a)

Deacons

The word "deacon," *diakonos*, is also sometimes translated "minister" and is used to describe Christ (Rom 15:8), Phoebe (Rom 16:1), Paul (1 Cor 3:5; 2 Cor 3:6), and Apollos (1 Cor 3:5). Paul addresses Philippians to the church in Philippi "with the bishops and deacons" (1:1). 1 Timothy 3:8-13 sets out the qualifications for holding the office.

> In the same way, servants [deacons] in the church should be dignified, not two-faced, heavy drinkers, or greedy for money. They should hold on to the faith that has been revealed with a clear conscience. They should also be tested and then serve if they are without fault. In the same way, women who are [deacons] in the church should be dignified and not gossip. They should be sober and faithful in everything they do. Servants [deacons] must be faithful to their spouse and manage their children and their own households well. Those who have served well gain a good standing and considerable confidence in the faith that is in Christ Jesus.

They perform functions like serving community meals (Acts 6:1-6) and caring for people in need (Acts 9:36-41).

The word sometimes translated "minister" is also *diakonos*. Sometimes, as in John 2:5, it refers to household servants, often those who serve at table. Much of the time, though, the word group refers specifically to Christian service. The verb *diakoneō*, "I serve," is prominent throughout the New Testament, beginning with such central passages as Mark 10:45, in which Jesus says of himself, "the Son of Man came not to be served but to serve, and to give his life a ransom for many" (NRSV; compare Matt 20:28; Luke 22:26-27). Jesus' life of service—healing, feeding, exorcizing, and so on—and his interpretation of his death as service means that all Christians see themselves as called to serve, not only deacons or ministers. John's Jesus says to the Twelve, "If I, your Lord and teacher, have washed your feet, you too must wash each other's feet" (13:14), and he tells Peter,

"Feed my lambs.... Take care of my sheep.... Feed my sheep" (21:15, 16, 17). Acts 6:1-5a draws the connection nicely:

> About that time, while the number of disciples continued to increase, a complaint arose. Greek-speaking disciples accused the Aramaic-speaking disciples because their widows were being overlooked in the daily food service [*diakonia*]. The Twelve called a meeting of all the disciples and said, "It isn't right for us to set aside proclamation of God's word in order to serve tables [*diakonein*]. Brothers and sisters, carefully choose seven well-respected men from among you. They must be well-respected and endowed by the Spirit with exceptional wisdom. We will put them in charge of this concern. As for us, we will devote ourselves to prayer and the service [*diakonia*] of proclaiming the word." This proposal pleased the entire community.

The Bible constantly urges Israel to care for the least among them, archetypically the resident aliens, orphans, and widows who are at greatest economic risk (Deut 4:29; Ps 68:5; Isa 10:2), but also anyone who is weak and vulnerable. "Poor persons will never disappear from the earth. That's why I'm giving you this command: you must open your hand generously to your fellow Israelites, to the needy among you, and to the poor who live with you in your land" (Deut 15:11). James 1:27 echoes the biblical tradition explicitly: "Religion that is pure and undefiled before God, the Father, is this: to care for orphans and widows in their distress, and to keep oneself unstained by the world" (NRSV). Acts depicts the early church in Jerusalem making a daily distribution of food to the widows among them and organizing a famine relief effort (11:29-30; cf. 2 Cor 8–9).[49]

Bishops

Bishops—or "overseers" (*episkopoi*, from which we get the word "episcopal")—appear as early as Philippians 1:1 and are mentioned in Acts 1:20; 20:28; 1 Timothy 3:1-7; Titus 1:7. In Acts 20:28 Paul addresses the Ephesian elders as overseers, apparently using the terms interchangeably.

> This saying is reliable: if anyone has a goal to be a supervisor [bishop] in the church, they want a good thing. So the church's supervisor [bishop] must be without fault. They should be faithful to their spouse, sober,

modest, and honest. They should show hospitality and be skilled at teaching. They shouldn't be addicted to alcohol or be a bully. Instead, they should be gentle, peaceable, and not greedy. They should manage their own household well—they should see that their children are obedient with complete respect, because if they don't know how to manage their own household, how can they take care of God's church? They shouldn't be new believers so that they won't become proud and fall under the devil's spell. They should also have a good reputation with those outside the church so that they won't be embarrassed and fall into the devil's trap. (1 Tim 3:1-7)

Just as overseers on wealthy estates are responsible for the efficient administration of the household, so bishops are responsible for the efficient— and faithful—administration of the church.

Widows

Toward the end of the first century, some women are identified as "widows" who exercise particular ministries of prayer and what we might call pastoral care within the church. Because they are supported by the church, they are free from the constraints of patriarchal households and the position is apparently so attractive that even unmarried women are joining the circle of widows, so it is not originally limited to women whose husbands have died. The Pastor finds the popularity of the office to be a financial burden on the church and seeks to impose restrictions on who may join:[50]

Take care of widows who are truly needy. But if a particular widow has children or grandchildren, they should first learn to respect their own family and repay their parents, because this pleases God. A widow who is truly needy and all alone puts her hope in God and keeps on going with requests and prayers, night and day. But a widow who tries to live a life of luxury is dead even while she is alive. Teach these things so that the families will be without fault. But if someone doesn't provide for their own family, and especially for a member of their household, they have denied the faith. They are worse than those who have no faith. Put a widow on the list who is older than 60 years old and who was faithful to her husband. She should have a reputation for doing good: raising children, providing hospitality to strangers, washing the feet of the saints, helping those in distress, and dedicating herself to every kind of good thing. But don't accept younger widows for the list. When their physical desires distract them from Christ, they will want to get married. Then they will be judged for setting aside their earlier commitment. Also, they learn to be lazy by going from house to house. They are not only lazy, but they also become gossips and busybodies, talking about things they shouldn't. So I want younger widows to marry, have children, and manage their homes so that they won't give the enemy any reason to slander us. (Some have already turned away to follow Satan.) If any woman who is a believer has widows in her family, she should take care of them and not burden the church, so that it can help other widows who are truly needy. (1 Tim 5:3-16)

It is noteworthy that these ecclesiastical titles all come from the realm of the household, because that reflects the physical context within which the earliest Christians gather: "deacon," "overseer," "elder," and "widow" all have their roots in the household. Servers (deacons) wait on householders and their families. Overseers (bishops) are high-status slaves who are entrusted with significant responsibilities in households. Elders are the most senior and revered members of families. Widows are defined by their marital status. It is scarcely surprising that, by the second century, the author of 1 Timothy and Titus begins to regularize qualifications for church officers, even though their roles are no longer restricted to domestic relationships.

Since these people are meeting in homes, we can imagine perhaps fewer than two dozen people at a time, so there is little need for much division of labor. It is perhaps inevitable, however, that the hosts of these Christian gatherings—the homeowners—seem sometimes to gain some prominence, whether or not they are the people who do the preaching, praying, prophesying, or speaking in tongues. Prisca and Aquila, a missionary couple on Paul's team, host churches in Corinth (Acts 18:2; Luke spells her name "Priscilla"), Ephesus (1 Cor 16:10), and Rome (Rom 16:3). The letter to Philemon is addressed also to "the church that meets in [his] house" (Phlm 1:2).

For Further Reading

Juel, Donald Harrisville. *Messiah and Temple: The Trial of Jesus in the Gospel of Mark.* Society of Biblical Literature Dissertation Series 31. Missoula, MT: Society of Biblical Literature, 1977.

Chapter 4

Jesus' Hands and Feet: The Church as the Body of Christ—and Other Bodies

The body of Christ is one of the most beloved images of the church. It is also one of the most debated, since for some interpreters it is not a metaphor at all but a statement of reality. That is, since the risen Christ is in heaven sitting at God's right hand, he has no body on earth except for the church that confesses him Lord. For Ernst Käsemann, for example, the image of the church as the body of Christ "is not a metaphorical figure of speech," because Paul asserts that "the exalted Christ really has an earthly body, and believers with their whole being are actually incorporated into it."[1] Eduard Schweizer similarly says the image is more than a metaphor, for "Christ himself *is* the body into which all members are baptized."[2] Such arguments, however, are shaped more by theological considerations than exegetical ones, since they obscure the fact that the word *body* is indeed functioning as a metaphor. We use the word *body* to describe a number of things: the body politic, a body of knowledge, bodies of water, and so on. In each of those cases, we are using the image of a living body—either human or animal—to think about something that does not have a body but can be thought of in terms of a body, particularly one that is united.

In the environment of the New Testament, the first person who uses the human body to talk about a community of people is Menenius Agrippa

Lanatus, a consul of the Roman Republic. According to the first-century CE historian Livy, Menenius persuaded some rebellious plebians in 494 BCE to end their attempt to secede by telling a story that uses the human body to talk about civic harmony and mutual interdependence.

> In the days when man's members did not all agree amongst themselves, as is now the case, but had each its own ideas and a voice of its own, the other parts thought it unfair that they should have the worry and the trouble and the labour of providing everything for the belly, while the belly remained quietly in their midst with nothing to do but to enjoy the good things which they bestowed upon it; they therefore conspired together that the hands should carry no food to the mouth, nor the mouth accept anything that was given it, nor the teeth grind up what they received. While they sought in this angry spirit to starve the belly into submission, the members themselves and the whole body were reduced to the utmost weakness. Hence it had become clear that even the belly had no idle task to perform, and was no more nourished than it nourished the rest, by giving out to all parts of the body that by which we live and thrive, when it has been divided equally amongst the veins and is enriched with digested food—that is, the blood. Drawing a parallel from this to show how like was the internal dissension of the bodily members to the anger of the plebs against the Fathers, [Menenius] prevailed upon the minds of his hearers. (Livy, *History of Rome* II.32.8–12)[3]

The "tale was designed to show the masses that the ruling classes, who appeared to be taking from them all the time, were in fact essential to the wellbeing of society, and the telling of this tale averted a revolt," observes Timothy Carter.[4] In ensuing years, a number of Greco-Roman authors similarly use the body to describe the properly functioning state. Plutarch (46–120 CE) writes an essay "On Brotherly Love" in which he describes a family as a body.[5] The image also appears in Dionysius of Halicarnassus (ca. 60 BCE–after 7 BCE), Philo of Alexandria (ca. 20 BCE–ca. 50 CE), Seneca the Younger (ca. 4 BCE–65 CE), and others to refer to a social unit, the state, or even the cosmos.[6] Margaret Mitchell draws attention to the many parallels in ancient political writings and concludes that, in 1 Corinthians 12, Paul reworks a common political metaphor and applies it to the church in Corinth.[7]

Paul's Use of the Body of Christ

The picture of the church as the body of Christ occurs only in the Pauline corpus, defined as Paul's letters and those letters written in his name by his theological descendants. The first use is in 1 Corinthians 12.[8]

> Christ is just like the human body—a body is a unit and has many parts; and all the parts of the body are one body, even though there are many. We were all baptized by one Spirit into one body, whether Jew or Greek, or slave or free, and we all were given one Spirit to drink. Certainly the body isn't one part but many. If the foot says, "I'm not part of the body because I'm not a hand," does that mean it's not part of the body? If the ear says, "I'm not part of the body because I'm not an eye," does that mean it's not part of the body? If the whole body were an eye, what would happen to the hearing? And if the whole body were an ear, what would happen to the sense of smell? But as it is, God has placed each one of the parts in the body just like he wanted. If all were one and the same body part, what would happen to the body? But as it is, there are many parts but one body. So the eye can't say to the hand, "I don't need you," or in turn, the head can't say to the feet, "I don't need you." Instead, the parts of the body that people think are the weakest are the most necessary. The parts of the body that we think are less honorable are the ones we honor the most. The private parts of our body that aren't presentable are the ones that are given the most dignity. The parts of our body that are presentable don't need this. But God has put the body together, giving greater honor to the part with less honor so that there won't be division in the body and so the parts might have mutual concern for each other. If one part suffers, all the parts suffer with it; if one part gets the glory, all the parts celebrate with it. You are the body of Christ and parts of each other. (12:12-27)

The image serves to underscore the indivisibility of the Corinthian community at the very moment Paul addresses multiple serious divisions within it: social and economic disparities, differences of theological conviction, varieties of religious experience, and competing personal loyalties, all of them exacerbated by commonly held cultural assumptions about who gets to determine community standards. In their world, it is the rich and powerful who get to say who is who and what is what, and Paul says instead that the revelation of God in Christ upends those assumptions. "The indicative of the metaphor points to the imperative of its application: all members of Christ's body must join together in honouring those with the least honour, a point Paul explicitly makes in v. 24."[9]

Perhaps Paul's most telling words are the ones that open the paragraph. "For just as the body is one and has many members, and all the members of the body, though many, are one body, so it is with Christ" (12:12 NRSV). In view of the conventional uses of the image of the body, one would expect Paul to say, "Just as the body is one and has many members, and all the members of the body, though many, are one body, so it is with the church." That is how Menenius's original story functions: just as the body has many parts, so it is with the Republic. Paul instead says the body is Christ, which means it is and is not a community like other communities. It is a community shaped by the person of Christ, the one

> who, though he was in the form of God,
>> did not regard equality with God
>> as something to be exploited,
> but emptied himself,
>> taking the form of a slave,
>> being born in human likeness.
> And being found in human form,
>> he humbled himself
>> and became obedient to the point of death—
>> even death on a cross. (Phil 2:6-8 NRSV)

The most important people are the weak and foolish, not the powerful and wise (1 Cor 1:18-25). It is no more possible for the elite in Corinth to dismiss the commoners among them than it is for the eye to say to the hand or the head to the feet, "I have no need of you" (1 Cor 12:21 NRSV). Paul does not say, "The eye *should not* say to the hand, 'I have no need of you,'" but "The eye *cannot* say to the hand, 'I have no need of you.'" It is not *possible* for the eye to dismiss the hand. The members of the body who deserve the greater honor are those who are the weakest and most dishonored. This is much like what Jesus says when he makes children, slaves, and marginal people the most important in the community.[10]

Throughout 1 Corinthians the word *body* recurs eighteen times, more frequently than in any other letter.[11] It refers variously to the bodies of individual believers, the body of Christ crucified and raised, the gathered body that is the church, and the bread the church shares at the Lord's Supper. These realities are deliberately mutually modifying. That is, the gathered community, made up of individuals, is always the body of Christ, which means it exists to exercise his ministry of love in the world and to "announce the Lord's death until he comes" (1 Cor 11:26 author translation). Sometimes the phrase refers only to Christ, specifically as he is crucified, rather than to the church: "Therefore, my brothers and sisters, you also died with respect to the Law through the body of Christ, so that you could be united with someone else. You are united with the one who was raised from the dead so that we can bear fruit for God" (Rom 7:4); "Isn't the cup of blessing that we bless a sharing in the blood of Christ? Isn't the loaf of bread that we break a sharing in the body of Christ?" (1 Cor 10:16). Later, Paul says much the same thing to the Romans, reprising the basic themes of his discussion in 1 Corinthians.

> Because of the grace that God gave me, I can say to each one of you: don't think of yourself more highly than you ought to think. Instead, be reasonable since God has measured out a portion of faith to each one of you. We have many parts in one body, but the parts don't all have the same function. In the same way, though there are many of us, we are one body in Christ, and individually we belong to each other. We have different gifts that are consistent with God's grace that has been given to us. (Rom 12:3-5)

The Body of Christ in Paul's Interpreters

The writer of Ephesians picks up Paul's metaphor a generation later and develops it still further. "[God's] purpose was to equip God's people for the work of serving and building up the body of Christ" (4:12).

> What is certain is that the image is used by Paul to exhort his readers to realize their unity, drawing upon their own awareness of their baptismal incorporation into the one body, and reminding them of the unity that

they share in partaking of the Lord's Supper. Moreover, his concept of the church as body goes beyond those uses of "body" as a social, corporate expression in Greco-Roman traditions, in which persons constitute a body through residence in a common polis. For Paul, the church is "the body of Christ." That is, it is not simply a body of persons who have a shared locale or interest. Nor is the phrase "of Christ" simply an identifying one. Paul employs a possessive genitive here. The body is Christ's own possession. Members do not create the body. Rather they are incorporated (a passive verb) by baptism into Christ and into his body and become subject to Christ's lordship.[12]

The body metaphor is emphatically organic and lends itself to expansion. The writers of Ephesians and Colossians develop it by further specifying that Christ is the head of his body. Whereas Paul says in 1 Corinthians 12 that the church as a body has a head and feet, hands and eyes, ears, a nose, and even "less honorable" parts, Ephesians and Colossians say the church is the body and Christ is its head. While certainly such a metaphor continues to exhort unity in the church, it further emphasizes the element of authority in Christ's headship. "God put everything under Christ's feet and made him head of everything in the church, which is his body. His body, the church, is the fullness of Christ, who fills everything in every way" (Eph 1:22-23). "You are one body and one spirit, just as God also called you in one hope. There is one Lord, one faith, one baptism, and one God and Father of all, who is over all, through all, and in all" (4:4-6).

> [Christ] is the head of the body, the church,
>   who is the beginning,
>   the one who is firstborn from among the dead
>   so that he might occupy the first place in everything.
> Because all the fullness of God was pleased to live in him,
>   and he reconciled all things to himself through him—
>   whether things on earth or in the heavens. (Col 1:18-20a)

The image is no longer local but universal, and Christ is the head of the body.[13] Individual congregations are encouraged to see themselves as parts of a global—even cosmic—whole.

The metaphor highlights unity and hides the matter of boundaries. It is difficult to think of adding to or taking away from a body. In fact, it is painful to contemplate. This is why it is such a compelling symbol of unity. It is very nearly coercive. "The eye *cannot* say to the hand, 'I have no need of you'" (1 Cor 12:21 NRSV, emphasis added). On the other hand, any given body, by definition, shares the same skin color and gender, which may not be particularly helpful to a church composed of people of many different sorts. The metaphor highlights unity but may also unintentionally point to uniformity.

Hebrews

The letter to the Hebrews urges its addressees to "Remember prisoners as if you were in prison with them, and people who are mistreated as if you were in their place" (13:3). The King James Version stays closer to the Greek here when it translates, "Remember them that are in bonds, as bound with them; and them which suffer adversity, as being yourselves also in the body."[14] The picture of solidarity in suffering is reminiscent of the parable of the sheep and the goats Matthew's Jesus tells: "I was in prison and you visited me" (25:36). Is the Pauline image echoed in the phrase in Hebrews "in the body"? It is apt if it is.

The Church as a Woman's Body

Sometimes the church is described as a particular body, specifically the body of a woman, rather than Christ's body.[15] Paul, his successor who wrote Ephesians, and John of Patmos all speak of the church as a woman married to Christ or to God. "As your father, I promised you in marriage to one husband. I promised to present you as an innocent virgin to Christ himself. But I'm afraid that your minds might be seduced in the same way as the snake deceived Eve with his devious tricks. You might be unable to focus completely on a genuine and innocent commitment to Christ" (2 Cor 11:2-3). Ephesians 5:25-32 prescribes proper Christian household order and compares the relationship between husband and wife to that between Christ and the church.

As for husbands, love your wives just like Christ loved the church and gave himself for her. He did this to make her holy by washing her in a bath of water with the word. He did this to present himself with a splendid church, one without any sort of stain or wrinkle on her clothes, but rather one that is holy and blameless.... No one ever hates his own body, but feeds it and takes care of it just like Christ does for the church because we are parts of his body.... Marriage is a significant allegory, and I'm applying it to Christ and the church. (Eph 5:25-27, 29, 32)[16]

In both these cases, the metaphor seeks to highlight the purity and faithfulness of the church to Christ and Christ's saving lordship over the church. It echoes the prophetic metaphor of God as Israel's husband (Hosea, Jeremiah, Ezekiel). This is inherently a dangerous metaphor when it includes violence against the wife, as Renita Weems demonstrates.[17]

Other Bodies: Plants and Animals

In the postindustrial twenty-first century, when the vast majority of Americans live in urban contexts, images like grapevines, olive orchards, flocks of sheep, and nets full of fish can seem a bit quaint. They were the stuff of everyday life for the ancients, though, and the New Testament employs a number of such metaphors to describe the people of God gathered around Jesus. They are not his body in the sense that the Body of Christ makes explicit; they are nevertheless bodies and each one evokes characteristics of the church.

Grapevines

"I am the vine," says Jesus, "you are the branches" (John 15:5). The intimacy of the image is immediately apparent, since branches cannot survive without a vine. It comes from the Bible, this picture of a grapevine. Isaiah uses it vividly:

> Let me sing for my loved one
> a love song for his vineyard.
> My loved one had a vineyard on a fertile hillside.
> He dug it,
> cleared away its stones,

> planted it with excellent vines,
>   built a tower inside it,
>   and dug out a wine vat in it.
> He expected it to grow good grapes—
>   but it grew rotten grapes.
> So now, you who live in Jerusalem, you people of Judah,
>   judge between me and my vineyard:
>   What more was there to do for my vineyard
>   that I haven't done for it?
> When I expected it to grow good grapes,
>   why did it grow rotten grapes?
> Now let me tell you what I'm doing to my vineyard.
> I'm removing its hedge,
>   so it will be destroyed.
> I'm breaking down its walls,
>   so it will be trampled.
> I'll turn it into a ruin;
>   it won't be pruned or hoed,
>   and thorns and thistles will grow up.
> I will command the clouds not to rain on it.
> The vineyard of the LORD of heavenly forces is the house of Israel,
>   and the people of Judah are the plantings in which God delighted.
> God expected justice, but there was bloodshed;
>   righteousness, but there was a cry of distress! (Isa 5:1-7)

Isaiah's Song of the Vineyard, as it is called, pictures God's faithful care of Israel, the people's repeated abandonment of the covenant, and God's promise of judgment. John 15:1-11 self-consciously echoes that: God removes the branches that do not bear fruit (v. 1) and promises that they will be destroyed (v. 6). Jesus also promises those who remain with him—that is, branches that stay connected to the vine—that they will bear fruit. "You didn't choose me, but I chose you and appointed you so that you could go and produce fruit and so that your fruit could last" (v. 16). What is this lasting fruit? Probably increasing numbers of people who believe in Jesus and who therefore share love for him and for one another. Lasting fruit may also refer to Christian communities that withstand hostility from their neighbors and remain faithful against the odds.

John is not the only evangelist who reprises Isaiah's metaphor of the vineyard. Matthew tells two parables in chapter 21, after the temple incident (vv. 12-17) evokes a serious challenge to Jesus' authority (vv. 23-27). The first concerns two sons whose father tells them to work in his vineyard (vv. 28-32). The first son agrees to go to work but does not; the second refuses but then does go to work. Jesus says the first son represents the Pharisaic leadership who profess to do God's will but do not believe in Jesus; the second stands for the "tax collectors and prostitutes" (v. 31) who repent and believe in Jesus. The vineyard here points to God's people who are either rightly served or not by their leaders.[18]

Matthew borrows the second parable in chapter 21, the wicked tenants, from Mark 12:1-12 and edits it to make it even more like Isaiah's Song of the Vineyard, because it is a terrible prediction of judgment on those who reject Jesus and conspire in his death:

> There was a landowner who planted a vineyard. He put a fence around it, dug a winepress in it, and built a tower. Then he rented it to tenant farmers and took a trip. When it was time for harvest, he sent his servants to the tenant farmers to collect his fruit. But the tenant farmers grabbed his servants. They beat some of them, and some of them they killed. Some of them they stoned to death. Again he sent other servants, more than the first group. They treated them in the same way. Finally he sent his son to them. "They will respect my son," he said. But when the tenant farmers saw the son, they said to each other, "This is the heir. Come on, let's kill him and we'll have his inheritance." They grabbed him, threw him out of the vineyard, and killed him. When the owner of the vineyard comes, what will he do to those tenant farmers? They said, "He will totally destroy those wicked farmers and rent the vineyard to other tenant farmers who will give him the fruit when it's ready." Jesus said to them, "Haven't you ever read in the scriptures, *The stone that the builders rejected has become the cornerstone. The Lord has done this, and it's amazing in our eyes* [Ps 118:22-23]? Therefore, I tell you that God's kingdom will be taken away from you and will be given to a people who produce its fruit. Whoever falls on this stone will be crushed. And the stone will crush the person it falls on." Now when the chief priests and the Pharisees heard the parable, they knew Jesus was talking about them. (Matt 21:33-45)

Colored as they all are by Isaiah's Song of the Vineyard, each of these New Testament pictures of the church as a vineyard carries a significant promise of judgment for failure to remain loyal to God's purposes. In John, the image of vine and branches is addressed to individuals in the community and urges them to be faithful to Jesus despite the pressure they receive from their neighbors to abandon him. In Matthew, the judgment is instead aimed at the Pharisaic leadership that competes with Matthew's community for converts.

Fields

In Mark 4, Jesus tells a string of parables that all have to do with surprising growth.[19] The parable of the sower (4:1-9), the light under a bushel (4:21-25), the seed growing secretly (4:26-29), and the mustard seed (4:30-32) all point to unexpectedly marvelous results from unimpressive beginnings. In the context of Jesus' ministry, they help explain how a backcountry rabbi can really be the Messiah of God. Although the allegorical interpretation of the parable of the sower (4:13-20) shifts attention away from the fields and toward the person of the sower, the rest of the parables highlight God's turning modest beginnings into magnificent conclusions. So also, the first-generation church gathered around Jesus may appear small and not particularly influential, but it is promised that God will make its life and ministry fruitful beyond all expectations.

Trees

As with so many of these images, the metaphor of God's people as a tree or trees comes from the Bible. Perhaps the best known is Psalm 1.

> Happy are those
>   who do not follow the advice of the wicked,
> or take the path that sinners tread,
>   or sit in the seat of scoffers;
> but their delight is in the law of the LORD,
>   and on his law they meditate day and night.
> They are like trees planted
>   [transplanted] by streams of water,

> which yield their fruit in its season,
>> and their leaves do not wither.
> In all that they do, they prosper.
>
> The wicked are not so,
>> but are like chaff that the wind drives away.
> Therefore the wicked will not stand in the judgment,
>> nor sinners in the congregation of the righteous;
> for the LORD watches over the way of the righteous,
>> but the way of the wicked will perish. (NRSV)

This tree is not simply thriving near a river, it is thriving despite being uprooted and transplanted. The verb translated "planted" in verse 3 really means "transplanted." This is a tree that, after having already grown and established roots somewhere, has been uprooted, moved, and replanted elsewhere. Ancient Near Eastern kings used to do just this with trees around the palaces of their vanquished enemies. They would uproot them and transplant them back at their own royal palaces as a type of victory garden—they bore witness to the "fruits" of the lands they had conquered, which means that the uprooting and transplanting of trees for the neo-Assyrians and Babylonians functions as a nice metaphor for what they did with human beings. The tree metaphor thus functions to depict God's people as restored after the exile.[20]

In a similar vein, Isaiah says of the exiles who return to their land, "They will be called Oaks of Righteousness, planted by the LORD to glorify himself" (61:3), and the Psalmist says, "But I am like a green olive tree in God's house; I trust in God's faithful love forever and always" (52:8) and "The righteous will spring up like a palm tree. They will grow strong like a cedar of Lebanon" (92:12). In each case, the trees thrive and demonstrate the loyalty of both God and the people to God's covenant.

Jeremiah, too, employs the image, particularly echoing Psalm 1, and also in an exilic context.

> They will be like trees planted by the streams,
>> whose roots reach down to the water.
> They won't fear drought when it comes;

> their leaves will remain green.
> They won't be stressed in the time of drought
> > or fail to bear fruit. (Jer 17:8)

> The LORD named you,
> "A blossoming olive tree, fair and fruitful";
> > but with the blast of a powerful storm
> > he will set it ablaze,
> > until its branches are completely consumed....

> I was like a young lamb led to the slaughter;
> I didn't realize that they were planning
> > their schemes against me:
> "Let's destroy the tree with its fruit;
> > let's cut him off from the land of the living
> > so that even any knowledge of him will be wiped out."
> (Jer 11:16, 19)

"Therefore, the LORD God proclaims: Of all the trees in the forest, I have decreed that the vine's wood is destined to be consumed by fire" (Ezek 15:6); "Then all the trees in the countryside will know that I, the LORD, bring down the tall tree and raise up the lowly tree, and make the green tree wither and the dry tree bloom. I, the LORD, have spoken, and I will do it" (Ezek 17:24).

Both Jesus and John the Baptist make use of the tree image to make similar points about how one's identity as a member of the people of God determines the sort of life one lives. This determination might be either individual or communal, that is, a person's identity or a community's. "In the same way, every good tree produces good fruit, and every rotten tree produces bad fruit. A good tree can't produce bad fruit. And a rotten tree can't produce good fruit. Every tree that doesn't produce good fruit is chopped down and thrown into the fire" (Matt 7:17-19). "Either consider the tree good and its fruit good, or consider the tree rotten and its fruit rotten. A tree is known by its fruit" (Matt 12:33). "The ax is already at the root of the trees. Therefore, every tree that doesn't produce good fruit will be chopped down and tossed into the fire" (Matt 3:10).

Paul makes a significantly different use of the tree metaphor in Romans 11:16-24. As he comes to the end of his long and complex argument about God's impartiality and abiding faithfulness to both Israel and the church (9:1–11:36), he thinks in terms of a tree. "If a root is holy, the branches will be holy too" (11:16). The tree is Israel, a cultivated olive tree, and God grafts Gentile Christian branches from a wild olive tree on to it by electing Gentiles in the same way God elects Israel—freely out of God's loving sovereignty and without regard to people's worthiness. Although it is a peculiar picture, since it is difficult to imagine why an arborist might graft wild branches on to a cultivated tree, it suits Paul's purposes well because it grants the priority of Israel as God's covenant people and the undisputed formerly pagan identity of non-Jewish Christians and at the same time affirms their equal status in the church. The image further paints a visual picture of the back-and-forth character of God's dealings with Israel and the church. God "trips up" Israel with the gospel of God's impartial righteousness (9:32b-33) as a means to call Gentiles into the church and when "the full number of the Gentiles comes in . . . all Israel will be saved" (11:25-26). He does not speculate about how God will accomplish such a feat; it is enough that he cannot imagine that human sin or hubris might be allowed to thwart God's saving intentions.

Sheep

"The LORD is my shepherd" (Ps 23:1) is the most familiar place in scripture where the people of God are compared to sheep, but the image is ubiquitous in the Hebrew Bible. Throughout the Ancient Near East, both deities and kings are referred to as shepherds, and that is true as well of Israel. Sheep and shepherds are a ubiquitous image in ancient Israel, partly, of course, because so much of the economy depends on herding sheep. The Psalmist says God

> chose his servant David,
>   and took him from the sheepfolds;
> from tending the nursing ewes he brought him
>   to be the shepherd of his people Jacob,
>   of Israel, his inheritance. (Ps 78:70-71 NRSV; 1 Sam 16:11-13)

70

Jeremiah says to the kings who have jeopardized Judah's security, "Woe to the shepherds who destroy and scatter the sheep of my pasture! says the LORD. . . . I will raise up shepherds over them who will shepherd them, and they shall not fear any longer, or be dismayed, nor shall any be missing, says the LORD" (23:1, 4 NRSV). The metaphor keeps shifting between human kings and God as king because in Israel, kings are never allowed to assume the quasi-divine status they hold elsewhere among Israel's neighbors (even though some of them try).

The New Testament refers most frequently to Jesus as shepherd, but on occasion the metaphor is used also to describe church leaders:

> Like shepherds, tend the flock of God among you. Watch over it. Don't shepherd because you must, but do it voluntarily for God. Don't shepherd greedily, but do it eagerly. Don't shepherd by ruling over those entrusted to your care, but become examples to the flock. And when the chief shepherd appears, you will receive an unfading crown of glory. In the same way, I urge you who are younger: accept the authority of the elders. (1 Pet 5:2-5a)

Matthew 9:36 is typical of the descriptions of Jesus. "Now when Jesus saw the crowds, he had compassion for them because they were troubled and helpless, like sheep without a shepherd." "If a shepherd has a hundred sheep, and one of them has gone astray, does he not leave the ninety-nine on the mountains and go in search of the one that went astray?" (Matt 18:12 NRSV). Jesus further describes God's people who need rescuing as lost sheep. "Go nowhere among the Gentiles, and enter no town of the Samaritans, but go rather to the lost sheep of the house of Israel. . . . I was sent only to the lost sheep of the house of Israel" (Matt 10:5-6; 15:24 NRSV).

In the Good Shepherd Discourse (John 10:1-32), Jesus not only calls his followers sheep, he says he is the (only) shepherd who cares for them and protects them from danger. In John 21:15-17, Jesus gives Peter a threefold opportunity to reverse the consequences of his threefold denial (18:17, 25, 27) by asking him, "Simon, son of John, do you love me?" (21:15, 16, 17). Each time, Peter responds that he does indeed love Jesus and Jesus commands him to "feed my lambs. . . . Take care of my sheep. . . . Feed my sheep." There is no particular difference here between lambs and sheep, and both describe Jesus' people whom God has given to him (17:6).[21]

Fish

When Jesus first approaches Simon and Andrew and James and John in Mark 1:16-20, he uses their vocations as fishermen to describe the new work he calls them to do.

> As Jesus passed alongside the Galilee Sea, he saw two brothers, Simon and Andrew, throwing fishing nets into the sea, for they were fishermen. "Come, follow me," he said, "and I'll show you how to fish for people." Right away, they left their nets and followed him. After going a little farther, he saw James and John, Zebedee's sons, in their boat repairing the fishing nets. At that very moment he called them. They followed him, leaving their father Zebedee in the boat with the hired workers.

Fishing is not a solitary activity, as we might imagine today with an individual person who wields a rod and reel to catch one fish at a time, but a decidedly corporate one. It takes several people to throw out and pull in fishing nets from a boat. Jesus speaks to the four men within their own contexts and calls them to a new one.

> The metaphor assures that the fishermen would retain their sense of social identity through a new livelihood that is mobile, profoundly relational, requiring unwavering skill and patience, and based on the Sea of Galilee and its environs. "Fishers of humans" thus conveys a vocation provided by Jesus. It has become clear that such a vocation is doing as Jesus does, namely, proclaiming the good news throughout Galilee.[22]

Luke 5:1-11 and John 21:1-14 tell similar stories about remarkable—indeed miraculous—catches of fish that include Jesus as well as the fishers he calls to himself and to the task of preaching. In both stories, a night of fruitless fishing is followed by Jesus' command to the disciples to cast their nets again, with the result that there are so many fish that the boats are threatened with sinking. The image underscores the divine source of the church's preaching—on their own, the disciples are unable to catch any fish at all—and the eschatological abundance promised in God's redemption. Matthew's Jesus tells a parable that shows the reverse side of the same phenomenon:

> Again, the kingdom of heaven is like a net that people threw into the lake and gathered all kinds of fish. When it was full, they pulled it to the shore, where they sat down and put the good fish together into containers. But the bad fish they threw away. That's the way it will be at the end of the present age. The angels will go out and separate the evil people from the righteous people, and will throw the evil ones into a burning furnace. People there will be weeping and grinding their teeth. (13:47-50)

Not every fish picked up in the church's nets will be faithful to Jesus, Matthew says. The church is a mixed community and not even the eschatological abundance God provides assures the single-minded devotion of God's people.[23]

Dough

Although modern translations of *zyme* frequently choose "yeast," a better translation is probably "leaven." "Leaven" refers to organic matter that causes fermentation.[24] In antiquity, bread dough was caused to rise by the addition of some uncooked dough from a previous batch. Yeast, as moderns know it, is a fungus that also causes fermentation, but it tends to be seen as measurable and manageable, whereas leaven has a reputation for being unpredictable. Like blood in the animal kingdom, leaven is seen as the life force in the plant kingdom, which is why we can watch it create life in a batch of dough. Ancient Israel celebrated the Feast of Unleavened Bread—Passover—in remembrance of the escape from Egypt and God's protection of them through the wilderness, and one of the critical activities associated with it is the cleansing out of all leaven in a house before the Passover bread can be baked (Exod 12:15). As a result, Paul sometimes uses leaven as a metaphor for something unclean to be removed from God's people. "But if part of a batch of dough is offered to God as holy, the whole batch of dough is holy too" (Rom 11:16). "Don't you know that a tiny grain of yeast [leaven] makes a whole batch of dough rise? Clean out the old yeast so you can be a new batch of dough, given that you're supposed to be unleavened bread. Christ our Passover lamb has been sacrificed, so let's celebrate the feast with the unleavened bread of honesty and truth, not with old yeast or with the yeast of evil and wickedness" (1 Cor 5:6-8).

New Creation

Twice Paul speaks of what he calls God's new creation.[25] "So if anyone is in Christ, there is a new creation: everything old has passed away; see, everything has become new!" (2 Cor 5:17 NRSV). "For neither circumcision nor uncircumcision is anything; but a new creation is everything!" (Gal 6:15 NRSV). John of Patmos does not use Paul's language exactly, but he too envisions God's redemption as a new creation, "a new heaven and a new earth" (Rev 21:1). John borrows an image from the prophet Isaiah about the day of God's victory: "Look! I'm creating a new heaven and a new earth: past events won't be remembered; they won't come to mind" (65:17; cf. 66:22). 2 Peter 3:13 similarly remembers Isaiah's new heaven and new earth when it speaks of the day of redemption.

This new creation or new heaven and earth is not intended to be seen as a categorically different reality than the heaven and earth that we know. Instead it is a picture of heaven and earth restored to the state in which God created them. The popular piety that separates heaven from earth and sees people as being "rescued" from the earth and transported to some disembodied heaven far from here misses the point of the New Testament's emphatic embrace of both heaven and earth. It is more like ancient pagan attitudes toward the absolute distinction between bodies and souls. Jews and Christians cannot imagine disembodied souls. The apocalyptic convictions about the new age that has dawned in Jesus' death and resurrection inspire the Christian community not only to look to the future day of redemption but also to resist conventional honor-shame and hierarchical social structures in the present.

As varied as all these bodies are, the metaphors all share a perspective on the church as singular. The oneness of a body calls for the oneness of a community. As the New Testament and two thousand years of church history attest, the church's unity is a precious quality that is constantly in jeopardy from any number of threats. A common quip among church people says, "Where two or three are gathered, there will be a schism."[26] From the very beginnings, Christians have interpreted Jesus' life, death, and resurrection from widely differing perspectives. The social and economic diversity in the church that from the start makes it so attractive to women and slaves almost immediately causes conflict. The varied religious and philosophical backgrounds Christians bring with them into the church inevitably cause them to hear preaching through multiple filters. This is why it is so remarkable that the church continues to long for the unity to which the metaphor of the body summons it.

For Further Reading

Martin, Dale B. *The Corinthian Body*. New Haven, CT: Yale University Press, 1995.

Minear, Paul S. *Christians and the New Creation: Genesis Motifs in the New Testament*. Louisville, KY: Westminster John Knox, 1994.

Chapter 5

Water Is Thicker Than Blood: The Church as Family

As with the metaphors of Israel and the temple, so the kinship metaphors for the church—brothers and sisters, parents and children, husbands and wives—seem to arise as early as the ministry of Jesus himself. Household imagery for the church seems to derive from Jesus' insistence that his followers are children of God, his symbolic replacement of his own family with his disciples, and subsequent Christian interpretation of baptism as adoption by God. The fact that Christian gatherings meet almost exclusively in private homes until well into the third century further reinforces the picture of the church as family.[1] "The dominant basis, focus, locus and model for the Jesus movement and its local assemblies was the household," says John Elliott.[2] There is a very real sense in which for Christians, to reverse the old adage, water is thicker than blood when it is the water of baptism.[3]

First a brief word about family life in Greco-Roman antiquity to set the context.[4] In the fourth century BCE Aristotle said,

> Now that it is clear what are the component parts of the state, we have first of all to discuss household management; for every state is composed of households. Household management falls into departments corresponding to the parts of which the household in its turn is composed; and the household in its perfect form consists of slaves and

77

freemen. The investigation of everything should begin with its smallest parts, and the smallest and principal parts of the household are master and slave, husband and wife, father and children. (*Politics* I.1253b)[5]

By nature, says Aristotle, people are either slaves or free people. Slavery is not a consequence of violent conquest or economic exploitation but of nature. So also—again, by nature—people are either male or female; by nature, men are superior to women just as free men rule their children and slaves. Children are not considered people until they reach the age of reason, and even then, male children are more human than female children, because they have more capacity for reason. This pyramidal structure of human experience is so taken for granted in antiquity that no one questions it. The man who heads a household has absolute authority over his wife, children, and slaves. The household, Aristotle says, is a "component part" of the state, and by the time of the first century, the empire is itself frequently referred to as a household, with the emperor as father and master. His provincial officials serve below him, the citizen class is below them, and noncitizens (the vast majority of people) stand beneath them. The divine realm is similarly described, particularly by Stoics, as headed by Zeus, with the other Olympians and the gods of other nations below him, and multiple spirits and forces below them.

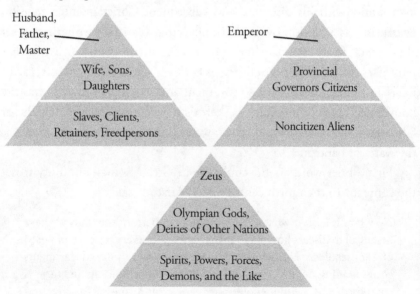

It is within such a highly stratified context that Christians make some unusual claims about themselves, their kinship relationships, and their life together as the church of Christ.

Children and Heirs of God

Every single New Testament writer refers to God as father and to believers as children of God. A few well-known examples will suffice to illustrate:

> Happy are people who make peace, because they will be called God's children. (Matt 5:9)

> Love your enemies, do good, and lend expecting nothing in return. If you do, you will have a great reward. You will be acting the way children of the Most High act, for he is kind to ungrateful and wicked people. (Luke 6:35)

> Those who did welcome [the Word],
>
> those who believed in his name,
>
> he authorized to become God's children. (John 1:12)

The Old Testament has a rather larger array of metaphors for God than the New Testament does. In addition to father (Isa 63:16), God is portrayed as mother (Hos 11:3-4; Isa 49:15), shepherd (Ps 23:1), rock (Deut 32:4), fortress (2 Sam 22:2), and so on. The New Testament has some diversity of images, too, but far less.[6] The dominant metaphor is father. Perhaps the most revealing reflection on how Christians become God's children is Paul's in Romans 8:14-23:

> All who are led by God's Spirit are God's sons and daughters. You didn't receive a spirit of slavery to lead you back again into fear, but you received a Spirit that shows you are adopted as his children. With this Spirit, we cry, "*Abba*,[7] Father." The same Spirit agrees with our spirit, that we are God's children. But if we are children, we are also heirs. We are God's heirs and fellow heirs with Christ, if we really suffer with him so that we can also be glorified with him. I believe that the present suffering is nothing compared to the coming glory that is going to be revealed to us.

The whole creation waits breathless with anticipation for the revelation of God's sons and daughters. Creation was subjected to frustration, not by its own choice—it was the choice of the one who subjected it—but in the hope that the creation itself will be set free from slavery to decay and brought into the glorious freedom of God's children. We know that the whole creation is groaning together and suffering labor pains up until now. And it's not only the creation. We ourselves who have the Spirit as the first crop of the harvest also groan inside as we wait to be adopted and for our bodies to be set free.

He says much the same thing to the Galatians: "Because you are sons and daughters, God sent the Spirit of his Son into our hearts, crying, '*Abba*, Father!' Therefore, you are no longer a slave but a son or daughter, and if you are his child, then you are also an heir through God" (Gal 4:6-7).[8]

The New Testament speaks remarkably frequently about Christians as God's heirs as well as children.[9] They are promised they will inherit nothing less than God's very kingdom, something that in Greco-Roman times can happen for only one son and only when the father dies. The fact that God never dies and all Christians inherit—both sons and daughters—points to an estate of riches vast beyond the imaginations of those who hear this remarkable news. In a world shaped by an ethic of scarcity, this picture of unlimited abundance is designed to reshape Christians' imaginations.[10]

Adoption

Adoption in antiquity is largely the province of the wealthy and takes place for one reason only: to secure an heir. Unlike today, when we adopt because we want to become parents by loving and nurturing children, a Greco-Roman landowner who does not have a son—or does not have a son he can trust to manage his estate faithfully—adopts a grown man he deems worthy of the role. For the most part, girl children who lose their parents or are abandoned are simply picked up by strangers in need of future slaves. As the adoptive mother of two daughters, I find this one of the strangest features of ancient life. The Greek comic dramatist Poseidippus (316–c. 250 BCE) quipped nearly three hundred years before the church:

Everyone, even if he is poor, rears a son,
But exposes a daughter, even if he is rich.[11]

When Pauline Christians—both male and female—come up out of the waters of baptism, however, they are all adopted by God, granted the privilege of addressing God as "*Abba*, Father."[12] Interestingly, Mark's Jesus uses that same phrase, "*Abba*, Father," at 14:36 when he prays to God about his impending arrest and execution. "*Abba*, Father, for you all things are possible. Take this cup of suffering away from me. However—not what I want but what you want." The words "of suffering" are not in the original, although that is clearly what the "cup" points to, and the juxtaposition of baptismal liturgy—"*Abba*, Father"—and communion liturgy—"this cup"—seems intended to remind Christian listeners that they will share Jesus' destiny, even as earlier in the story Jesus assures James and John, "The cup that I drink you will drink; and with the baptism with which I am baptized, you will be baptized" (10:39 NRSV).[13]

Jesus is repeatedly described as God's Son, often as the "firstborn son" (Luke 2:7, 23; Rom 8:29; Col 1:15, 18; Heb 1:6; Rev 1:5). In Johannine Christianity he is emphatically God's "only son" (John 1:14, 18; 3:16, 18; 1 John 4:9). That means he is the legitimate heir to God's kingdom. That the church should share Jesus' inheritance is nothing short of remarkable. Paul says,

> We know that God works all things together for good for the ones who love God, for those who are called according to his purpose. We know this because God knew them in advance, and he decided in advance that they would be conformed to the image of his Son. That way his Son would be the first of many brothers and sisters. (Rom 8:28-29)

Hebrews goes even further to call the entire church "the assembly of God's firstborn children who are registered in heaven" (12:23), further bending the metaphor almost beyond recognition, since one can scarcely have multiple "firstborn" children, even though God does.

This exalted status as God's children that Christians are granted at baptism stands in stark contrast to the social status most of them possess in their own communities. Although we know that the early church included some prominent people, for the most part they were people of modest means and low status. Paul reminds the Corinthians, "Look at your situation when you were called, brothers and sisters! By ordinary human standards not many were wise, not many were powerful, not many were from the upper class" (1 Cor 1:26). This contrast between their perceived identities as children of God and the ways they are treated by their family members and neighbors who consider them socially disruptive and disrespectful of common values creates a sense of dissonance that helps them see themselves and their communities as both part of the world and separate from it as they are members of the household of God.[14]

The Church as Alternative Family

For all that he is part of a renewal movement and a reformer of Israel's worship of God, Jesus is also portrayed as creating a family around himself. When he gives symbolic names to Peter, James, and John (Mark 3:16-17) he is acting as a father, for it is the father's responsibility in antiquity to name children. Mark, at least, understands the action that way, for in the next breath he narrates a shocking story in which Jesus replaces his family of origin—his mother and brothers who are afraid he is out of his mind—with those who do God's will (3:19b-35). Jesus' mother and siblings are cast alongside Jesus' enemies. They are as hostile to him as are the scribes from Jerusalem.

> After his family heard, they went out to seize him because they kept saying, "He is beside himself." And the scribes who came down from Jerusalem kept saying, "He has Beelzebul," and, "He casts out demons by the power of the chief demon." (3:21-22 author translation)[15]

This is an alarming scenario and interpreters ancient and modern have devoted great quantities of imagination and ink to the family's defense. Matthew and Luke remove Mark 3:21 altogether from their versions of the story, and various translations of it see someone other than Jesus' relatives restrain him or question his emotional stability:[16]

> And when his <u>friends</u> heard *of it*, they went out to lay hold on him: for <u>they</u> said, "He is beside himself." (KJV)

82

And when His <u>own people</u> heard of *this*, they went out to take custody of Him; for <u>they</u> were saying, "He has lost His senses." (NASB)

When his <u>family</u> heard it, they went out to restrain him, for <u>people</u> were saying, "He has gone out of his mind." (NRSV)

When his <u>family</u> heard what was happening, they came to take control of him. <u>They</u> were saying, "He's out of his mind!" (CEB)

Still others translate so that people do not think that Jesus is out of control but that the crowd is, either because it is so enthusiastic or because it is so hostile.[17] Surely, it has seemed to many readers, Mark 3:21 cannot possibly mean what it says, that Jesus' family considers his ministry demonic or delusional.

> Matthew and Luke…narrate the story of Jesus' true kinfolk to say that he enlarges his family to include those who do God's will. Mark's version, by contrast, excludes Jesus' family of origin because they oppose him as his enemies do, and it replaces them with the fictive kinship of the household of faith.[18]

Something remarkably similar happens at Mark 6:1-6 where Jesus preaches in the synagogue in Nazareth and the townsfolk are scandalized that he has left his mother and brothers and sisters behind to go off gallivanting around the countryside. "They were repulsed by him and fell into sin" (6:3). This is followed immediately by his gathering the Twelve again to himself and commissioning them to do exactly what he has been doing (6:7-13). "They cast out many demons, and they anointed many sick people with olive oil and healed them" (6:13). The disciples demonstrate that they are Jesus' family because they join the "family business."

Jesus calls God "father" and calls his disciples to do likewise,[19] which makes them brothers and sisters. He predicts that, as a consequence, their families of origin will be torn asunder by divided loyalties: "Brothers and sisters will hand each other over to be executed. A father will turn his child in. Children will defy their parents and have them executed. Everyone will hate you on account of my name" (Matt 10:21-22; cf. Mark 13:12).[20] "And everyone who has left houses or brothers or sisters or father or mother or children or fields, for my name's sake, will receive a hundredfold, and will inherit eternal life" (Matt 19:29 NRSV; cf. Mark 10:29-30; Luke 18:29). "Whoever comes to me and does not hate father and mother, wife and children, brothers and sisters, yes, and even life itself, cannot be my disciple" (Luke 14:26 NRSV). "You will be betrayed even by parents and brothers, by relatives and friends; and they will put some of you to death" (Luke 21:16 NRSV).

> Do not think that I have come to bring peace to the earth; I have not come to bring peace, but a sword.
>
> For I have come to set a man against his father,
> and a daughter against her mother,
> and a daughter-in-law against her mother-in-law;
> and one's foes will be members of one's own household.
>
> Whoever loves father or mother more than me is not worthy of me; and whoever loves son or daughter more than me is not worthy of me; and whoever does not take up the cross and follow me is not worthy of me. Those who find their life will lose it, and those who lose their life for my sake will find it. (Matt 10:34-39 NRSV)

This sounds nothing like what people refer to as "traditional family values"! Instead it profoundly redefines them. It is not unusual, though, to hear of people in Greco-Roman antiquity whose changes in religious loyalty result in domestic disruption. The primary obligation of the *paterfamilias*, the "father of the family" or "head of the household," after assuring the family's wealth and honor, is to oversee its proper religious observances. These include particularly veneration of the family's ancestors and participation in the cults of the city, often including worship of the emperor. When people become Christians, though (or Jews, for that matter), they become monotheists. They are the only people in the Empire who reject all gods but their own, and Romans find this behavior not only intolerant but also dangerous. To reject the gods, it is thought, risks bringing their wrath on the entire community. Paul says the Thessalonian Christians "turned to God from idols" (1 Thess 1:9), so they can no longer participate in their families' household shrines or worship in the civic temples. One poignant picture of a convert to Judaism who becomes estranged from her family is the first- or second-century Jewish novel *Joseph and Asenath*, which expands on the story in Genesis 41:45 where the Pharaoh gives to the patriarch Joseph Asenath, daughter of the Egyptian priest Potiphera, as a reward for his service and loyalty.[21]

Paul

"Brothers and sisters" is Paul's favorite designation for the recipients of his letters. He uses it sixty-five times in Romans, 1 and 2 Corinthians, Galatians, Philippians, and 1 Thessalonians, more than all other terms of direct address put together. In addition to being these people's brother, Paul is also their father. In 1 Corinthians 4:15-16 he says, "You may have ten thousand mentors in Christ, but you don't have many fathers. I gave birth to you [a better translation is 'I became your father'] in Christ Jesus through the gospel, so I encourage you to follow my example." He similarly tells Philemon he became Onesimus's father when Onesimus became a Christian (Phlm 10). It is rather common in antiquity for teachers to think of themselves as the fathers of their students. The *Pirke Aboth*, for example, are the "sayings of the fathers," a collection of Jewish ethical maxims that are part of the Mishnah, gathered perhaps at the end of the first century CE.[22] Similarly, pagan philosophers often refer to themselves as the fathers of their students. In the Greco-Roman world, fathers are responsible for the educations of their sons—and sometimes even daughters—so the metaphor is ready at hand to moral and religious teachers.[23]

Surprisingly, Paul also sometimes speaks of himself as the mother of his churches. In 1 Corinthians 3:2 he says, "I gave you milk to drink instead of solid food, because you weren't up to it yet." This is no small feat in a world in which infant formula and baby bottles have not yet been invented. Only a woman who has given birth can give milk to a baby, whether it is her own child or the child of her master or mistress, in which case she is a wet nurse. To the Galatians he says something even more shocking. "My little children, I'm going through labor pains again until Christ is formed in you" (Gal 4:19).[24] In both these contexts, as Beverly

Gaventa demonstrates, Paul is dealing with the lives of his churches and his relationships with them. He uses paternal imagery to talk about his establishment of congregations and switches to maternal imagery when he discusses the intimacy and nurture of the ongoing relationships he seeks to develop or repair. That he considers himself in labor with the Galatian church for a second time highlights the great jeopardy his relationship with them faces.

Paul's most telling employment of kinship metaphors is in 1 Thessalonians 2, where he combines both maternal and paternal images with other familial relationships. He is reminding the Thessalonians of what happened when he and his coworkers lived among them and first preached to them.

> For we never came with a word of flattery, just as you know, nor in a pretext for greed—God is witness—nor were we seeking glory from human beings, whether from you or from others, although we were able to throw our weight around as apostles of Christ. Instead we became *infants*[25] in your midst, as if a *wet nurse*[26] might care tenderly for her own *children*; thus since we longed for you we were pleased to share with you not only the gospel of God but also our own lives, because you became beloved to us. For you remember, *brothers and sisters*, our labor and toil, because night and day we worked in order not to put any weight on you as we preached to you the gospel of God. You are witnesses, as is God, how we came in a holy and just and blameless manner to you who believe, just as you know how, as a *father* with his own *children*, we comforted and encouraged and bore witness to each one of you in order that you might walk in a manner worthy of the God who calls you into his own kingdom and glory....But when we were *orphaned* from you for a season, *brothers and sisters*—in person not in heart—with great desire we spared no effort to see your face. (2:5-12, 17 author translation)

In rehearsing his relationship with the Thessalonians, Paul calls them his brothers and sisters, as he does so frequently, and further describes himself and his coworkers as the church's newborn baby, their wet nurse, and their father—and all in the same paragraph. A paragraph later, he says his separation from them is like being orphaned from them.

Although each of these metaphors—infant, wet nurse, child, sibling, father, and orphan—carries its own weight, when they occur so close together they create a context that modifies them all. An infant is helpless, vulnerable, and powerless, a startling image for apostles of Christ who are "able to throw [their] weight around" (v. 7). Some manuscripts of verse 7 read *ēpioi* ("gentle") rather than *nēpioi* ("infants") because some ancient scribes (and not a few modern interpreters) think it inappropriate for Paul to call himself a baby and much more appropriate to say he is gentle.[27] The two words are spelled the same except for the first letter, and that letter is also the last letter of the preceding word. The possibilities that scribes copying the letter could make mistakes are many. The evidence is clear, though. The best and more numerous manuscripts read *nēpioi*, "infants." The likelihood is greater that scribes would change a metaphor that makes a reader scratch her head—"infants"—into an easy-to-understand adjective—"gentle"—than the reverse. This means that Paul is deliberately mixing metaphors here. In a single phrase he refers to himself as both the newborn and the wet nurse who breastfeeds the baby. This is what Gaventa calls a "metaphor squared."[28] The two images mutually modify each other so as to say that the apostles and the church have an intimate relationship marked by love, nurture, and trustworthiness that is alternately caring and cared for. Each depends on the other: "we were pleased to share with you not only the gospel of God but also our own lives, because you became beloved to us," he says (v. 8). His absence from them makes him feel like an orphan (v. 17).

Eugene Boring argues that this language "is not merely descriptive or hortatory but also performative: it brings into being the reality it describes."[29] The fact that the apostles are mothers and fathers of the church as well as its children and siblings destabilizes the conventional hierarchy that structures Greco-Roman households. Matters of authority, power, and obedience simply do not look the same when mutuality and role reversals like these are in play. The church as a family looks nothing like a conventional Roman household because it is formed in the image of Christ who,

> though he was in the form of God,
>> did not regard equality with God
>> as something to be exploited,
> but emptied himself,
>> taking the form of a slave,
>> being born in human likeness.
> And being found in human form,
>> he humbled himself
>> and became obedient to the point of death—
>> even death on a cross. (Phil 2:6-8 NRSV)

In a community shaped by the cross, there is no room for measuring status or jockeying for power. "Do nothing from selfish ambition or conceit, but in humility regard others as better than yourselves" (Phil 2:3 NRSV); "love one another with mutual affection; outdo one another in showing honor" (Rom 12:10 NRSV).

Families within the Church

We have seen how frequently the first Christians find their families of origin disrupted by their professions of faith in Jesus. It is clear, though, that not all of them abandon parents and spouses and children permanently to follow Jesus. In Mark, Jesus calls his first disciples, Simon, Andrew, James, and John away from their family fishing businesses (1:16-20), but Simon's mother-in-law shows up only two paragraphs later when Jesus heals her of a fever and she promptly cooks them all dinner (1:29-34). James and John are repeatedly identified as the sons of Zebedee, even after they leave their father with the boat (3:17; 10:35). In Matthew, their mother makes an appearance to ask that her sons sit at Jesus' left and right hand in his glory (Matt 20:20) and she watches Jesus' crucifixion with the other women (27:56). Luke changes the story of Jesus' summoning the fishermen to include a miraculous catch of fish that will sustain the families when their sons leave home to join Jesus (Luke 5:1-11). Jesus repeatedly invokes the fifth commandment to honor father and mother.[30] After he raises Jairus's daughter from the dead, he tells her parents to feed her (Mark 5:43). Jesus

88

forbids divorce (Mark 10:11-12), which is unprecedented in any human society we know of, and even quotes Genesis 1:27 and 2:24 approvingly:

> But from the beginning of creation, "God made them male and female." "For this reason a man shall leave his father and mother and be joined to his wife, and the two shall become one flesh." So they are no longer two, but one flesh. Therefore what God has joined together, let no one separate. (Mark 10:6-9 NRSV)

The result of prohibiting divorce, which is provided for and regulated in scripture and limited to men's initiative (Deut 24:1), is a radical reenvisioning of marriage that keeps women from being disposable when men want to trade up. It sets a new standard for faithfulness that is a hallmark of the church.

Jesus' welcome of children, much to the disgruntlement of his disciples, and his description of children as model disciples, is another example of reordered family values. Mark 10:13-16 immediately follows the prohibition of divorce with these words:

> People were bringing children to Jesus so that he would bless them. But the disciples scolded them. When Jesus saw this, he grew angry and said to them, "Allow the children to come to me. Don't forbid them, because God's kingdom belongs to people like these children. I assure you that whoever doesn't welcome God's kingdom like a child will never enter it." Then he hugged the children and blessed them.

We who are more influenced by Victorian family values than Greco-Roman ones are inclined to think of children as innocent, untouched by the world, and trusting. The ancients instead thought that children were not yet fully human and that they were therefore powerless and without status, much like women or slaves. When Jesus makes children the model disciples, then, he reverses conventional assumptions and upends social order. The *paterfamilias* of the church is the God who raised Jesus from the dead, which means that the most important people in the household are the least honored—children, women, and slaves.[31]

There is no mere replacement here of families of origin with the church family in early Christianity. Domestic relations are clearly transformed, however. Nowhere do we see this more plainly than in Paul's letters. In 1 Corinthians 7, Paul addresses questions the Corinthians have posed to him in a letter of their own. "Now concerning the matters about which you wrote: 'It is well for a man not to touch a woman'" (v. 1 NRSV). Why in the world would they say such a thing? Apparently because Paul himself told them the very thing. One of the more foreign-sounding things to modern ears about Paul is his preference for celibacy over marriage. Repeatedly in this chapter he says that, although marriage is permissible to Christians, celibacy is better (7:7, 8, 25-40). This sounds odd coming from a Jew who knows full well that the first commandment God gave to human beings was to "be fruitful and multiply" (Gen 1:28 NRSV).

As an apocalyptic Jew of the first century, however, Paul has a greatly modified view of sex and marriage. There are other Jews we know of—the Qumran covenanters,[32] for instance, and the philosophically minded Therapeutae[33]—who similarly eschew marriage not simply as a form of self-denial but as a way to maintain a state of ritual purity required to stand in God's presence. The Bible makes clear that, although sex is a good thing and provides children who carry on one's name, sex is not holy. It is a common part of life, and there is a vital distinction between things that are holy and things that are common. "You are to distinguish between the holy and the common, and between the unclean and the clean," says Leviticus 10:10 (NRSV). What is unclean is not immoral or evil; it is simply common. It prevents one from engaging God who is holy. Leviticus 15 details multiple rituals for restoring one's cleanliness—the capacity to enter God's presence—after sexual intercourse. Even childbirth, much as it is to be welcomed and celebrated, renders mothers temporarily unclean. Leviticus 12:2 says the birth of a son renders a mother unclean for seven days; verse 5 says the birth of a daughter makes her unclean for fourteen days.

Because sex is so fraught with commonness, it is not surprising that soldiers engaged in a war on God's behalf—sometimes called a War of Yahweh—abstain from sex. Deuteronomy 23:9-14 says,

> When you are encamped against your enemies you shall guard against any impropriety. If one of you becomes unclean because of a nocturnal emission, then he shall go outside the camp; he must not come within

the camp. When evening comes, he shall wash himself with water, and when the sun has set, he may come back into the camp. You shall have a designated area outside the camp to which you shall go. With your utensils you shall have a trowel; when you relieve yourself outside, you shall dig a hole with it and then cover up your excrement. Because the LORD your God travels along with your camp, to save you and to hand over your enemies to you, therefore your camp must be holy, so that he may not see anything indecent among you and turn away from you.

This is what makes the story in 2 Samuel 11 so bitterly ironic. King David, who thinks he is entitled to whatever he wants when he wants it, commits adultery with his neighbor Bathsheba, who is married to Uriah the Hittite, a soldier in David's army fighting a war on God's behalf, a War of Yahweh. Bathsheba becomes pregnant and David attempts to cover the tracks of his sin by summoning Uriah to the palace. He tells him, "Go down to your house, and wash your feet" (probably a euphemism for "have sex with your wife"), in hopes that the child Bathsheba carries will be taken for Uriah's own (v. 8 NRSV). Uriah is more faithful to David—and to God—than David is, though, and he remains at David's house. In a fit of pique, David sends Uriah back to the most dangerous part of the battle, where he is killed, and the king takes the widowed Bathsheba as his wife (v. 27). David's failure to observe the requirements of holy war highlights the seriousness with which others—particularly apocalyptic Jews—take them.

In the first century, Paul and the Qumran covenanters think of themselves as warriors for God. They are engaged in a battle of cosmic proportions against Satan and his armies, and they anticipate God's cataclysmic intervention at any moment to defeat Satan and usher in God's realm. For Paul and other apocalyptic Christians, that intervention has already been inaugurated in the death and resurrection of Jesus, which makes the moment more urgent than ever. This is why celibacy is so important to him. He must be ready at any moment for Christ to come on the clouds and gather his elect. Jesus, too, seems to have shared the perspective, at least to a certain extent. In answering a question from Sadducees who do not believe in resurrection, he says, "when [people] rise from the dead, they neither marry nor are given in marriage, but are like angels in heaven" (Mark 12:25 NRSV). Since angels are always in God's presence, they too abstain from sex.

The subject of celibacy is apparently one Paul raises with other churches, as well. He reminds the Thessalonians of instructions he has previously given them about how to "obtain one's own vessel in holiness and honor" (1 Thess 4:4 author translation). This is a metaphor that has elicited a number of interpretations. Just what is the "vessel" everyone is supposed to know how to acquire? The CEB and NRSV render the phrase "control your own body," since the word "vessel" is sometimes used elsewhere to refer to a human body. Alternatively, the RSV says "take a wife for himself," despite the fact that this completely contradicts what Paul says in 1 Corinthians 7. The KJV stays closest to Paul's language when it says, "possess his vessel." Jouette Bassler makes a compelling case for looking at 1 Thessalonians 4:1-12 alongside 1 Corinthians 7:36-38 and instead reading "acquire one's own vessel" as "acquire one's own celibate partner."[34] The apostolic exhortation, then, is that Christians know how to acquire a celibate partner much as he tells the Corinthians:

> If someone thinks he is acting inappropriately toward an unmarried woman whom he knows ["his own virgin"], and if he has strong feelings and it seems like the right thing to do, he should do what he wants—he's not sinning—they should get married. But if a man stands firm in his decision, and doesn't feel the pressure, but has his own will under control, he does right if he decides in his own heart not to marry the woman. Therefore, the one who marries the unmarried woman ["his own virgin"] does right, and the one who doesn't get married will do even better.

The phrase "his own virgin" in 1 Corinthians 7:36, 38 echoes "his own vessel" in 1 Thessalonians 4:4. Such unconventional relationships—partnerships that produce no offspring—draw the attention of the church's neighbors and bring widespread criticism. Paul points to that in the rest of chapter 4 when he says,

> You don't need us to write about loving your brothers and sisters because God has already taught you to love each other. In fact, you are doing loving deeds for all the brothers and sisters throughout Macedonia.

Now we encourage you, brothers and sisters, to do so even more. Aim to live quietly, mind your own business, and earn your own living, just as I told you. That way you'll behave appropriately toward outsiders, and you won't be in need. (vv. 9-12)

One consequence of that social hostility in later generations is a retreat from Paul's radical views of kinship and a reimposition of conventional domestic morality in the church. Five times we encounter what are called household codes that reflect the pagan virtue of a hierarchical household headed by a *paterfamilias*. Ephesians 5:22–6:9; Colossians 3:18–4:1; 1 Peter 2:13–3:7; 1 Timothy 2:8–3:1a; and Titus 2:1-10 all sound very much like what we read in popular philosophical discussions of household order.[35] The husband/father/master is called to rule his wife, children, and slaves and they are to obey him. This reflects a conviction that order in the household reflects order in the church, which reflects order in the universe. The motivation is not, as in Aristotle's *Politics*, that domestic order is natural. Instead, Christian household codes invoke God's authority, even though the expected behaviors are not materially different from pagan ethics.

One of these household codes comes across as more nuanced and complicated than the others. First Peter 3 suggests that another community, clearly reflecting Paul's influence, knows and shares his provision for religiously motivated celibacy within marriage.

Wives, likewise, submit to your own husbands. Do this so that even if some of them refuse to believe the word, they may be won without a word by their wives' way of life. After all, they will have observed the reverent and holy manner of your lives. Don't try to make yourselves beautiful on the outside, with stylish hair or by wearing gold jewelry or fine clothes. Instead, make yourselves beautiful on the inside, in your hearts, with the enduring quality of a gentle, peaceful spirit. This type of beauty is very precious in God's eyes. For it was in this way that holy women who trusted in God used to make themselves beautiful, accepting the authority of their own husbands. For example, Sarah accepted Abraham's authority when she called him master. You have become her children when you do good and don't respond to threats with fear. Husbands, likewise, submit by living with your wife in ways that honor her, knowing that she is the weaker partner. Honor her all the more, as she is also a coheir of the gracious care of life. Do this so that your prayers won't be hindered. (1 Peter 3:1-7)

Paul commends temporary abstinence in order for married couples to devote themselves to prayer (1 Cor 7:5). First Peter similarly urges that Christian men make a home together with their Christian wives in such a way that their prayers not be hindered (1 Pet 3:7). Christian husbands, on the other hand, are exhorted to "make a home together according to knowledge as with the weaker feminine vessel." That word "vessel" is the same one Paul uses to describe the celibate partners he urges the Thessalonians to acquire (1 Thess 4:4). The context in 1 Peter is that some Christian women are married to non-Christian men who are not likely to take well to their wives' devotion to celibacy. The same dynamic can be seen in a roughly contemporary but noncanonical text, *The Acts of Paul*.[36] The book tells of Paul's preaching about "abstinence and the resurrection" and details his successful conversion of a woman named Thecla whose fiancé is not happy when she informs him there will be no sex in their marriage. He proceeds to accuse Paul of forbidding marriage (cf. 1 Tim 4:3) and gets him thrown in jail. Thecla, who has cut her hair and wears men's clothing in order to be a traveling evangelist like Paul, goes to him in prison and bribes the jailer to let him escape.

If the feminine vessels are weaker, presumably the masculine vessels are stronger, but stronger in what regard? It is likely that the relative strength of men and women in marriage refers to their capacities to resist and control passion. Women are widely seen in antiquity as more susceptible to passion than men are. Thus married couples in the Pauline orbit refer to each other as "vessels," and as Paul says believers should know how to acquire their own vessels in holiness and honor (1 Thess 4:4), so 1 Peter tells Christian husbands to pay honor to their weaker feminine vessels (1 Pet 3:7). Marriage, however, tempts wives to adorn themselves to please their husbands rather than to please God, so both Paul and 1 Peter advise against such incitement to passion (1 Cor 7:31-34; 1 Pet 3:3, 5). A further connection between 1 Pet 3:1-7 and Paul's advice concerns the attitude a Christian woman should take toward a non-Christian husband. Paul says she stands to "sanctify" or even to "save" her husband (as a Christian man does his non-Christian wife) if she remains in the marriage (1 Cor 7:14, 16). First Peter says a Christian woman has an opportunity to "win" her unbelieving husband by her socially conventional and pious demeanor (3:1).[37]

The advantages of kinship metaphors for the church are many. A family is organic rather than organizational, just as the body image is. Unlike the body, however, a family can welcome an unlimited number of new members. The earliest uses of the metaphor, with their replacement of conventional pagan domestic morality with the radical unity and nonhierarchical relationships, are most life-giving in a church that is frequently tempted to conform itself to the prevailing culture.

The weaknesses of the family image, however, are also easy to see. If, as becomes the case relatively early, the clergy are portrayed as fathers of their families, the relationships can all too easily become abusive, particularly when traditional family values replace the apocalyptic convictions Paul espouses.

The Oscar-winning film *Places in the Heart*[38] is set in a small town in Depression-era eastern Texas. A young white widow with two children takes in an African American hobo who teaches her what she needs to know about growing cotton so she can save her home from foreclosure. She also rents a room to a blind, embittered World War I veteran who slowly comes out of his isolation to help the struggling family stave off disaster. The film explores numerous themes of family and kinship, both positive and negative. In the final scene, Edna and her children are in church—the same sanctuary where the movie's initial scene takes place—with many characters in the story: her sister and adulterous (but now forgiven) brother-in-law, the greedy and heartless banker who wants her farm and who foists his disabled brother on her to get him out of his own home, the Klansmen who have violently driven her savior Moze out of town because he shamed the white cotton farmers for bringing in the first bale of cotton. After the preacher preaches and the choir sings, they begin to share the Lord's Supper, and strange things begin to happen. Children take communion, something that would not have happened in a Protestant church in the 1930s; some of the African Americans who have helped Edna pick cotton are communing with white folks, another historical anachronism; even Moze, who has already left town, is there. The last two people we see sitting by Edna are her dead husband, now very much alive, and the young black man who accidentally killed him and who was lynched early in the story, also alive. This is not a picture of Edna's family; it is a picture of God's family.

For Further Reading

Johnson, E. Elizabeth. "Life Together in the Household of God." In *Shaking Heaven and Earth: Essays in Honor of Walter Brueggemann and Charles B. Cousar.* Edited by Christine Roy Yoder, Kathleen M. O'Connor, E. Elizabeth Johnson, and Stanley P. Saunders. Louisville, KY: Westminster John Knox, 2005 89–103.

Minear, Paul S. *Images of the Church in the New Testament.* Philadelphia: Westminster, 1960. 165–72.

Notes

Introduction

1. N. T. Wright, *Paul and the Faithfulness of God* (Minneapolis: Fortress, 2013), 826.

2. Barbara E. Reid, OP, "What's Biblical about the Church?" *Bible Today* 46 (2008): 189.

3. Georg Strecker, *Theology of the New Testament*, ed. Friedrich Wilhelm Horn, trans. M. Eugene Boring (Berlin: DeGruyter, 1996), 181.

4. Philadelphia: Westminster, 1960.

5. "Preface," in Paul S. Minear, *Images of the Church in the New Testament*, foreword by Leander E. Keck (repr. Louisville, KY: Westminster John Knox, 2004), xi. See Avery Dulles's *Models of the Church* (Garden City, NY: Doubleday, 1974; expanded ed., Garden City, NY: Image Books, 1987).

6. Jaroslav J. Pelikan, *Luther the Expositor* (Saint Louis: Concordia, 1959), 5.

7. See Michael Jinkins, *The Church Faces Death: Ecclesiology in a Post-Modern Context* (New York: Oxford University Press, 1999).

8. See Linda Mercadante, *Belief without Borders: Inside the Minds of the Spiritual but Not Religious* (New York: Oxford University Press, 2014).

9. Alfred Firmin Loisy, *The Gospel and the Church*, trans. Christopher Hume (Philadelphia: Fortress, 1976; orig., 1902), 166.

10. Rudolf Bultmann, *Theology of the New Testament*, trans. Kendrick Grobel (Waco, TX: Baylor University Press, 2007; orig., 1948), 33.

11. "A public or semipublic dining venue, such as a restaurant building, would cohere with the ability of 'outsiders and unbelievers' (1 Cor 14:23) to enter into the community gathering" (Edward Adams, "Placing the Corinthian Communal Meal," in *Text, Image, and Christians in the Graeco-Roman World: A Festschrift in Honor of David Lee Balch*, ed. Aliou Cissé Niang and Carolyn Osiek, Pittsburgh Theological Monograph Series 176 [Eugene, OR: Pickwick, 2012], 30); Peter Oakes, *Reading Romans in Pompeii: Paul's Letter at Ground Level* (Minneapolis: Fortress, 2009).

12. L. Michael White, *From Jesus to Christianity: How Four Generations of Visionaries & Storytellers Created the New Testament and Christian Faith* (New York: HarperCollins, 2004), 442.

13. Matt 28:1; Mark 16:2; Luke 24:1; John 20:1, 19; Acts 20:7.

14. William V. Harris, *Ancient Literacy* (Cambridge: Harvard University Press, 1991).

15. Wallace Martin, "Metaphor," in *The New Princeton Encyclopedia of Poetry and Poetics*, ed. A. Preminger et al. (Princeton, NJ: Princeton University Press, 1993), 760.

16. George Lakoff and Mark Johnson, *Metaphors We Live By*, second ed. (Chicago: University of Chicago Press, 2003; orig., 1980); see also Timothy Bahti, "Figure, Trope, Scheme," in Preminger et al., *New Princeton Encyclopedia of Poetry and Poetics*, 409–12; Lynn R. Huber "Knowing Is Seeing: Theories of Metaphor Ancient, Medieval, and Modern," in *Like a Bride Adorned: Reading Metaphor in John's Apocalypse*, Emory Studies in Early Christianity (New York: T & T Clark 2007), 45–88. Jeffery Donaldson moves beyond Lakoff and Johnson to say that the virtually limitless variety of metaphors has its own

fruitfulness (*Missing Link: The Evolution of Metaphor and the Metaphor of Evolution* [Montreal: McGill-Queen's University Press, 2015]).

17. Frederick Christian Bauerschmidt, "God as Author: Thinking Through a Metaphor," *Modern Theology* 31 (2015): 574. The words are from Donne's Meditation 17 in *Devotions upon Emergent Occasions and Death's Duel* (New York: Oxford University Press, 1987; orig., 1624).

18. Beverly Roberts Gaventa, "Our Mother St. Paul: Toward the Recovery of a Neglected Theme," *Princeton Seminary Bulletin* 17 (1996): 39.

19. C. Lynn Nakamura, "Monarch, Mountain, and Meal: A Traditio-Historical Investigation of the Eschatological Banquet of Isaiah 24:21-23; 25:6-10a" (PhD diss., Princeton Theological Seminary, 1992).

20. Paul Ricoeur, *The Conflict of Interpretations* (Evanston, IL: Northwestern University Press, 1974), 288, 299.

1. The People of God

1. "Biblical" here refers to the Bible of the early Christians, what most Christians today know as the Old Testament. Although no official action had yet been taken to canonize the Hebrew scriptures, already in the first century Pharisaic Jews like Jesus and his first followers recognized a threefold collection of authoritative writings that later came to be known as the Law, the Prophets, and the Writings, in Hebrew, *Tanak*. See Luke 24:44: "Then he said to them, 'These are my words that I spoke to you while I was still with you—that everything written about me in the law of Moses, the prophets, and the psalms must be fulfilled.'"

2. Nicholas Campion, *Astrology and Cosmology in the World's Religions* (New York: New York University Press, 2012), 136.

3. See Frank S. Frick, "The Tribes," in *The HarperCollins Bible Dictionary*, ed. Paul J. Achtemeier et al. (San Francisco: HarperSanFrancisco, 1985), 1175–77; C. J. H. Wright, "Family," in *Anchor Bible Dictionary*, ed. David Noel Freedman, vol. 2 (New Haven, CT: Yale University Press, 1992), 761–69; Richard D. Nelson, "Tribe," in *The New Interpreter's*

Dictionary of the Bible, ed. Katharine Doob Sakenfeld (Nashville: Abingdon, 2009), 665–68.

4. Ephraim and Manasseh are really Joseph's sons (Gen 41:50-52) whom Jacob adopts on his deathbed: "Jacob said to Joseph, 'God Almighty appeared to me in Luz in the land of Canaan. He blessed me and said to me, "I am about to give you many children, to increase your numbers, and to make you a large group of peoples. I will give this land to your descendants following you as an enduring possession." Now, your two sons born to you in the land of Egypt before I arrived in Egypt are my own. Ephraim and Manasseh are just like Reuben and Simeon to me'" (48:3-5).

5. Raymond E. Brown, "*Episkopē* and *Episkopos*: The New Testament Evidence," *Theological Studies* 41, no. 2 (1980): 324.

6. See John 1:47; Acts 2:22; 3:12; 5:35; 7:23; 13:16; 21:28; Rom 9:4, 6; 11:1; 2 Cor 11:22; Phil 3:5.

7. I am indebted to Martinus C. deBoer, who first helped me think about these shifts in a lecture at Princeton Theological Seminary in 1984.

8. See E. Mary Smallwood, *The Jews under Roman Rule: From Pompey to Diocletian: A Study in Political Relations,* second ed. (Leiden: Brill, 1981); Louis H. Feldman, *Jew and Gentile in the Ancient World: Attitudes and Interactions from Alexander to Justinian* (Princeton, NJ: Princeton University Press, 1996).

9. God-fearers: Luke 7:4-5; Acts 10:2, 7; 13:43, 50; 16:14; 17:7, 17; 18:7; proselytes: Matt 23:15; Acts 2:10; 13:43.

10. See Timothy H. Lim, *Holy Scripture in the Qumran Commentaries and Pauline Letters* (Oxford: Clarendon, 1997), 127.

11. John Calvin, *Institutes of the Christian Religion* II.XV.6, ed. John T. McNeill, trans. Ford Lewis Battles (Philadelphia: Westminster, 1967), 501.

12. See Jacob Neusner, *From Politics to Piety: The Emergence of Pharisaic Judaism* (New York: Ktav, 1979); Ellis Rivkin, *A Hidden Revolution: The Pharisees' Search for the Kingdom Within* (Nashville: Abingdon, 1978).

13. John H. Hayes and Sara R. Mandell, *The Jewish People in Classical Antiquity: From Alexander to Bar Kochba* (Louisville, KY: Westminster John Knox, 1998).

14. *The Old Testament Pseudepigrapha*, ed. James H. Charlesworth, 2 vols. (New York: Doubleday, 1983).

15. E.g., Matt 2:23; Acts 24:25.

16. J. Louis Martyn, *History and Theology in the Fourth Gospel*, third ed. (Louisville, KY: Westminster John Knox Press, 2003; orig., 1968), 62.

17. See James D. G. Dunn, *The Partings of the Ways between Christianity and Judaism and Their Significance for the Character of Christianity* (London: SCM, 1991).

18. Michael E. Fuller, *The Restoration of Israel: Israel's Re-gathering and the Fate of the Nations in Early Jewish Literature and Luke–Acts* (Berlin: De Gruyter, 2006).

19. Although there are two times in Matthew's Gospel where Jesus speaks about "my church" and "the church" (16:18; 18:17), those words come from the evangelist rather than from Jesus. The word occurs nowhere else in the Gospels. Stanley P. Saunders (*Preaching the Gospel of Matthew: Proclaiming God's Presence* [Louisville, KY: Westminster John Knox, 2010], 178) argues that Matthew's uses of *ekklēsia* are not particularly "Christian." They simply refer to the disciples as an assembly in a generic sense.

20. John P. Meier, *A Marginal Jew: Rethinking the Historical Jesus*, vol. 2, *Mentor, Message, and Miracles* (New York: Doubleday, 1994).

21. For good introductions to how the Gospels came to be, see M. Eugene Boring, *An Introduction to the New Testament: History, Literature, Theology* (Louisville, KY: Westminster John Knox, 2012), and Warren

Carter, *Telling Tales about Jesus: An Introduction to the New Testament Gospels* (Philadelphia: Fortress, 2016).

22. Mark repeatedly uses the same verb, *ekballō*, to describe what Jesus does to the demons throughout Mark.

23. Matthew changes Mark's "forty days" to "forty days and forty nights" (Matt 4:2) to recall not only Israel's wilderness wanderings but also Moses' "forty days and forty nights" on Mount Sinai receiving the law from God (Exod 24:18). See John P. Meier, *The Vision of Matthew: Christ, Church and Morality in the First Gospel* (New York: Crossroad, 1991), 59–60.

24. Matt 4:1-11; Luke 4:1-13.

25. The word "fishers" sounds a bit quaint but is deliberately chosen to remind us that these men fished with nets, not rods and reels or spears. See Blake E. Wassell and Stephen R. Llewelyn, "'Fishers of Humans,' the Contemporary Theory of Metaphor, and Conceptual Blending Theory," *Journal of Biblical Literature* 133 (2014): 627–46.

26. John P. Meier, "The Disciples of Christ: Who Were They?" *Mid-Stream* 38 (1999): 131. Wassell and Llewelyn note that "Mark 1:16-20 alludes to 1 Kings 19:19-21, Elijah's call of Elisha, in several ways: (1) the teacher chooses the disciples and not they him; (2) the disciples are engaged in their occupation and leave it as a result of the teacher; (3) the use of *opisō* ['after']" ("Fishers of Humans," 632, n. 14).

27. My translation. Some manuscripts of Mark add the words "whom he also named apostles" in v. 14 after "he made Twelve." That is the work of later scribes who tried to harmonize Mark's story with Luke's version of it in Luke 6:13. See Joel Marcus, *Mark 1–8*, Anchor Bible (New York: Doubleday, 2000), 263.

28. It is curious that the Gerasene demoniac, after his demons are exorcized, begs also to be "with him," but Jesus instead sends him home to his people to report what has happened (5:18).

29. Ernst Käsemann, "The Problem of the Historical Jesus," in *Essays on New Testament Themes*, trans. W. J. Montague (London: SCM, 1964; orig., 1954).

30. *Rocky*, dir. John G. Avildsen (1976; United Artists).

31. Marcus, *Mark 1–8*, 179.

32. 1 Cor 1:12; 3:22; 9:5; 15:5; Gal 1:18; 2:7-9, 11, 14.

33. See Raymond E. Brown, Karl P. Donfried, and John Reumann, eds., *Peter in the New Testament: A Collaborative Assessment by Protestant and Roman Catholic Scholars* (Minneapolis: Augsburg, 1973); Pheme Perkins, *Peter: Apostle for the Whole Church*, Studies on Personalities in the New Testament (Columbia: University of South Carolina Press, 1994); Markus Bockmuehl, *Simon Peter in Scripture and Memory: The New Testament Apostle in the Early Church* (Grand Rapids: Baker Academic, 2012).

34. Marcus, *Mark 1–8*, 265.

35. R. Alan Culpepper, *John, the Son of Zebedee: The Life of a Legend*, Studies on Personalities in the New Testament (Columbia: University of South Carolina Press, 1994).

36. The Gospels are all written for readers—or listeners—who already know the story of Jesus' life, death, and resurrection.

37. John P. Meier, "The Circle of the Twelve: Did It Exist during Jesus' Public Ministry?" *Journal of Biblical Literature* 116 (1997): 635–72; Meier, "The Disciples of Christ: Who Were They?" 129–35.

38. Matt 10:5; 26:20, 47; Mark 3:16; 4:10; 6:7; 9:35; 10:32; 11:11; 14:10, 20, 43; Luke 8:1; 9:1, 12; 18:31; 22:3, 47; John 6:67, 70, 71; 20:24; Acts 6:2; 1 Cor 15:5.

39. In Acts, Luke uses the word "disciple" in a more general sense to refer to Christians (Acts 6:1-2, 7; 9:1, etc.).

40. John Dominic Crossan, *The Historical Jesus: The Life of a Mediterranean Jewish Peasant* (San Francisco: HarperSanFrancisco, 1991), 401.

41. That is, sources that have no literary relationship with each other (Mark, John, and Paul, for instance) independently mention them.

42. John 13:23; 19:26; 20:2; 21:7; 21:20. For a discussion of the many theories offered for the identity of "the disciple whom Jesus loved," see Richard Bauckham, *The Testimony of the Beloved Disciple: Narrative, History, and Theology in the Gospel of John* (Grand Rapids: Baker Academic, 2007).

43. Matthew, Mark, and Luke can be looked at together, synoptically, because they share literary relationships.

44. George B. Caird and Lincoln D. Hurst, *New Testament Theology* (New York: Oxford University Press, 1994), 101.

45. Meier, "The Circle of the Twelve," 658.

46. David L. Bartlett, *Christology in the New Testament*, Core Biblical Studies (Nashville: Abingdon, 2017), 7.

47. Meier, "The Circle of the Twelve," 658.

48. Meier, "The Circle of the Twelve," 657.

49. Scot McKnight, "Jesus and the Twelve," *Bulletin for Biblical Research* 11 (2001): 218.

2. A Fraught Metaphor

1. Further on the following, see E. Elizabeth Johnson, "Jews and Christians in the New Testament: John, Matthew, and Paul," *Reformed Review* 42 (1988–89): 113–28.

2. E. Elizabeth Johnson, *The Function of Apocalyptic and Wisdom Tradition in Romans 9–11*, Society of Biblical Literature Dissertation Series 109 (Atlanta: Scholars Press, 1989); Johnson, "God's Covenant Faithfulness to Israel," in *Reading the Letter to the Romans*, ed. Jerry L. Sumney, SBL Resources for Biblical Studies (Atlanta: Scholars Press, 2012), 157–68.

3. J. Louis Martyn, *Galatians: A New Translation with Introduction and Commentary*, Anchor Bible 33A (New York: Doubleday, 1997), 565, 567.

4. Matt 4:23; 9:35; 10:17; 12:9; 13:54.

5. As Hans Küng suggests, the same thing might be said of any group of Jews in the first century: Pharisees, Sadducees, Essenes, or Zealots (*The Church*, trans. Ray Ockenden and Rosaleen Ockenden [New York: Burns and Oates, 1968], 108).

6. The mention of "other sheep" that do not belong to the evangelist's fold at 10:16 may suggest a mixed congregation, as does the arrival of the Greek tourists in 12:20.

7. For a very accessible and nuanced treatment of the phrase *the Jews*, see Jaime Clark-Soles, "'The Jews' in the Fourth Gospel" in *Feasting on the Gospels: John*, vol. 1, ed. Cynthia A. Jarvis and E. Elizabeth Johnson (Louisville, KY: Westminster John Knox, 2015), xi–xiv.

8. J. Louis Martyn, *History and Theology in the Fourth Gospel*, A New Testament Library Classic, rev. and expanded (Louisville, KY: Westminster John Knox, 2003; orig., 1979).

9. My translation.

10. Luke Timothy Johnson, *The Letter of James: A New Translation with Introduction and Commentary*, Anchor Bible 37A (New York: Doubleday, 1995), 170–71.

11. It is interesting that Paul uses the same language from Hosea 1:6, 9 to describe both Israel and the Gentiles in Rom 9:25-26. A good bit of 1 Peter seems to reflect familiarity with Paul's letters.

12. Steven Richard Bechtler, *Following in His Steps: Suffering, Community, and Christology in 1 Peter*, Society of Biblical Literature Dissertation Series 162 (Atlanta: Society of Biblical Literature, 1998).

13. The list of names most resembles those in Gen 35:22-26 and Gen 49, although Manasseh replaces Dan.

14. Brian Blount, *Revelation: A Commentary*, New Testament Library (Louisville, KY: Westminster John Knox, 2009), 102–3, 132, 143.

15. "It is possible that the word 'Nicolaitans' is allegorical, Nicolas being simply the Greek equivalent of Balaam (cf. Rev 2:14), arrived at by a fanciful etymology, and that the persons referred to in Revelation had no real existence as a sect. A Gnostic sect of this name, however, is alluded to by Irenaeus, Clement of Alexandria, and Pseudo-Tertullian; and Irenaeus affirms that they were founded by the Nicolas of Antioch mentioned in Acts 6:5, though this is perhaps no more than a conjecture" ("Nicolaitans," in *The Oxford Dictionary of the Christian Church*, ed. F. L. Cross and E. A. Livingstone, third rev. ed. [Oxford: Oxford University Press, 2005], 1152). See also Elisabeth Schüssler Fiorenza, "Apocalyptic and Gnosis in the Book of Revelation and Paul," *Journal of Biblical Literature* 92 (1973): 565–81.

16. Jeffrey S. Siker, *Disinheriting the Jews: Abraham in Early Christian Controversy* (Louisville, KY: Westminster John Knox, 1991). The original title of the book was "The Making of Orphans: The Use of Abraham in Early Christian Controversy with Judaism from Paul through Justin Martyr" (PhD diss., Princeton Theological Seminary, 1988). See also Rosemary Radford Ruether, *Faith and Fratricide: The Theological Roots of Anti-Semitism* (New York: Seabury, 1979); Stephen G. Wilson, *Related Strangers: Jews and Christians 70–170 C.E.* (Minneapolis: Fortress, 1995); Judith Lieu, *Image & Reality: The Jews in the World of the Christians in the Second Century* (Edinburgh: T & T Clark, 1996).

17. *Shoah*, dir. Claude Lanzmann (1985; Criterion Collection, 2013 Blu-ray).

18. Claude Lanzmann, *Shoah: The Complete Text of the Acclaimed Holocaust Film*, preface by Simone de Beauvoir (Boston: Da Capo, 1995; orig., 1985), 89.

19. See Anatoly Liberman, "Why Don't We Know the Origin of the Word Ghetto?" on the Oxford University Press blog, "Oxford Etymologist," March 4, 2009, for a discussion of the possible etymology of the word (http://blog.oup.com/2009/03/ghetto/; accessed July 31, 2016). Although it does not determine the origin of *ghetto*, see Daniel

B. Schwartz, *Ghetto: The History of a Word* (Cambridge, MA: Harvard University Press, 2019), which traces the various uses of the term across multiple cultures over time.

20. Raul Hilberg, *The Destruction of the European Jews*, 3 vols., rev. ed. (New York: Holmes & Meier, 1985), 1:8–9.

21. Yossi Klein Halevi, "Israel Commentary," January 15, 2003 (http://www.israel-commentary.org/archives/000005.html; accessed June 1, 2016). See also Halevi, *At the Entrance to the Garden of Eden: A Jew's Search for Hope with Christians and Muslims in the Holy Land* (New York: HarperCollins, 2002). To choose only two representative Protestant statements, see Presbyterian Church (USA), *A Theological Understanding of the Relationship between Christians and Jews* (Louisville, KY: Presbyterian Distribution Services, 1987); and Reformed Church in America, "A Study of the Biblical Perspective on the Evangelization of the Jews for the RCA Today" in *The Church Speaks: Papers of the Commission on Theology, Reformed Church in America, 1959–1984*, ed. James I. Cook, Historical Series of the RCA 15 (Grand Rapids: Eerdmans, 1985), 101–12. For an Orthodox perspective see Harold Smith, "Supersession and Continuance: The Orthodox Church's Perspective on Supersessionism," *Journal of Ecumenical Studies* 49, no. 2 (2014): 247–73.

22. Wayne Gilbert Rollins, *Jung and the Bible* (Atlanta: John Knox Press, 1983), 4.

23. *The Christian Imagination: Theology and the Origins of Race* (New Haven, CT: Yale University Press, 2010). Susan Sontag similarly highlights the ethical implications of metaphors when she examines the ways people speak about tuberculosis, cancer, and AIDS (*Illness as Metaphor and AIDS and Its Metaphors* [New York: Farrar, Strauss, and Giroux, 1988]).

24. Küng, *The Church*, 115, 119–25.

3. God's House and Priesthood

1. Michael B. Hundley, *Gods in Dwellings: Temples and Divine Presence in the Ancient Near East*, Writings from the Ancient World Supplements

(Atlanta: Society of Biblical Literature, 2013), 3. See also his *Keeping Heaven on Earth: Safeguarding the Divine Presence in the Priestly Tabernacle* (Tübingen: Mohr Siebeck, 2011).

2. Annie Dillard, *Teaching a Stone to Talk: Expeditions and Encounters* (New York: Harper & Row, 1982), 40–41.

3. Brennan W. Breed, Old Testament Interpretation Lecture, Columbia Theological Seminary, Decatur, Georgia, 2016.

4. See Jacob Milgrom, *Leviticus: A New Translation with Introduction and Commentary*, Anchor Bible (New York: Doubleday, 2001).

5. William P. Brown, *The Seven Pillars of Creation: The Bible, Science, and the Ecology of Wonder* (New York: Oxford University Press, 2010), 36–40; Brown, *Character in Crisis: A Fresh Approach to the Wisdom Literature of the Old Testament* (Grand Rapids: Eerdmans, 1996), 40.

6. Stanley P. Saunders, "A Dwelling Place for God: Recovering the Forgotten Story of God, Humankind, Temple, and Creation," the Jackson B. Davidson Memorial Lecture on Science and Religion, First Presbyterian Church, Oak Ridge, Tennessee (April 24, 2014); http://www.fpcor.org/pdfs/SaundersLectureTEXT.pdf (accessed June 16, 2016).

7. Jon D. Levenson, "Temple and World," *Journal of Religion* 64, no. 3 (1984): 285.

8. Anthony J. Saldarini, "Holiness," in *The HarperCollins Bible Dictionary*, ed. Paul J. Achtemeier et al. (San Francisco: HarperSanFrancisco, 1996), 431.

9. Cf. Ezra 2:63; Neh 7:65.

10. In 1 Sam 4:6-8 Israel's enemies similarly recognize the ark as the very presence of God. "When they learned that the ark of the LORD had come to the camp, the Philistines were afraid; for they said, 'Gods have come into the camp.' They also said, 'Woe to us! For nothing like this has happened before. Woe to us! Who can deliver us from the power of

these mighty gods? These are the gods who struck the Egyptians with every sort of plague in the wilderness'" (NRSV).

11. See Joshua R. Porter, "Ark," in Achtemeir, *HarperCollins Bible Dictionary*, 70–71.

12. For more, see Carol L. Meyers, "The Temple" in Achtemeier, *HarperCollins Bible Dictionary*, 1096–1105.

13. For more, see Meyers, "The Temple," 1104.

14. See Ira Brent Driggers, "The Politics of Divine Presence: Temple as Locus of Conflict in the Gospel of Mark," *Biblical Interpretation* 15, no. 3 (2007): 227–47.

15. See also Luke 2:41-51; 4:1-13; 18:9-14; 19:45–20:8; 21:1-38; 23:45; Acts 3:1-26; 4:1; 5:20-26, 42; 21:26-30; 22:17; 24:6, 12, 18; 25:8.

16. Matthew tells the same stories, although he separates the fig tree and temple episodes rather than leaving them woven together as in Mark (Matt 21:12-17, 18-22). Luke also tells the story of the temple incident, but significantly without the cursing of the fig tree (19:45-48).

17. James S. Hanson, *The Endangered Promises: Conflict in Mark*, Society of Biblical Literature Dissertation Series 171 (Atlanta: Scholars Press, 2000), 196.

18. This is what makes Pilate's release of Barabbas so bitterly ironic in Mark, because Barabbas is really a brigand and Jesus is not: Barabbas has "committed murder during an uprising" (15:7). Barabbas's name means "son of the father," which makes his release even more ironic, since the reader knows that Jesus is the true "son of the father," that is, God (cf. Mark 1:11; 9:7; 15:39).

19. For example, Isa 20; Jer 19; Ezek 2:8–3:6.

20. Dale B. Martin, "Jesus in Jerusalem: Armed and Not Dangerous," *Journal for the Study of the New Testament* 37, no. 1 (2014): 9.

21. See here Donald Harrisville Juel, *Messiah and Temple: The Trial of Jesus in the Gospel of Mark*, Society of Biblical Literature Dissertation Series 31 (Missoula, MT: Society of Biblical Literature, 1977).

22. Matt 22:44; 26:64; Mark 12:36; 14:62; Luke 20:42; 22:69; Acts 2:33-34; 5:31; 7:55-56; Rom 8:34; 1 Cor 15:25-28; Eph 1:20; Col 3:1; Heb 1:3, 13; 8:1; 10:12; 12:2; 1 Pet 3:22.

23. See David M. Hay, *Glory at the Right Hand: Psalm 110 in Early Christianity*, Society of Biblical Literature Monograph Series 18 (Nashville: Abingdon, 1973).

24. J. R. Daniel Kirk, "Time for Figs, Temple Destruction, and Houses of Prayer in Mark 11:12-25," *Catholic Biblical Quarterly* (2012): 509–10.

25. Adela Yarbro Collins, *Mark: A Commentary*, Hermeneia (Minneapolis: Fortress, 2007), 11.

26. Donald Harrisville Juel, *A Master of Surprise: Mark Interpreted* (Minneapolis: Fortress, 1994), 35–36.

27. In Col 2:11, the word differentiates two sorts of circumcision: "You were also circumcised by him. This wasn't performed by human hands—the whole body was removed through this circumcision by Christ."

28. Similarly, Matthew says of Jesus' authoritative interpretation of scripture, "I tell you, something greater than the temple is here" (12:6 NRSV).

29. Rom 1:7; 1 Cor 1:2; 2 Cor 1:1; Phil 1:1.

30. Georg Strecker, *Theology of the New Testament*, ed. Friedrich Wilhelm Horn, trans. M. Eugene Boring (Berlin: DeGruyter, 1996), 179.

31. See Raymond F. Collins, *The Many Faces of the Church: A Study in New Testament Ecclesiology* (New York: Crossroad, 2003), 33–37.

32. Jill E. Marshall, "Community Is a Body: Sex, Marriage, and Metaphor in 1 Corinthians 6:12–7:7 and Ephesians 5:21-33," *Journal of Biblical Literature* 134 (2015): 843.

33. Richard B. Hays, *First Corinthians*, Interpretation (Louisville, KY: Westminster John Knox, 2011), 108–9.

34. Strecker, *Theology of the New Testament*, 179.

35. Psalm 118:22 is quoted also at Matthew 21:42; Mark 12:10; Luke 20:17 when Jesus foreshadows his death in the parable of the laborers in the vineyard. Luke further has Peter say, "This Jesus is the stone you builders rejected; he has become the cornerstone!" (Acts 4:11).

36. My translation. See E. Elizabeth Johnson, *The Function of Apocalyptic and Wisdom Traditions in Romans 9–11*, Society of Biblical Literature Dissertation Series 109 (Atlanta: Scholars Press, 1989), 154–55. Cf. Leander E. Keck, who argues instead that the stone of stumbling is the law of God (*Romans*, Abingdon New Testament Commentaries [Nashville: Abingdon, 2005], 244–45). The reason other modern translators read "the one who has faith in *him*" (CEB) or "whoever believes in *him*" (NRSV) is that they assume Paul is using the same collection of "stone" verses that includes Psalm 118:22, words that are notably absent in Romans 9.

37. Gard Granerød, "Melchizedek in Hebrews 7," *Biblica* 90, no. 2 (2009): 188.

38. In John, it is instead Jesus' raising Lazarus from the dead that precipitates his arrest, trial, and execution (11:16, 53-57).

39. John A. T. Robinson suggests that John intends to say that the temple not made with hands is both the church and Jesus' body (*The Body: A Study in Pauline Theology*, Studies in Biblical Theology 1 [London: SCM, 1957], 5). That seems unlikely, though, in view of the fact that throughout the Fourth Gospel Jesus himself replaces not only the temple but also all the festivals of Judaism (Passover—2:13, 23; 4:45; 6:4; 11:55; 12:1, 12, 20; 13:1, 29; 18:28, 39; 19:14; Sukkoth—7:1–14:37; Hannukkah—10:22). He is greater than Israel's patriarchs (4:12; 8:53) and even the law of God (1:17).

40. Paul S. Minear, *Images of the Church in the New Testament* (Philadelphia: Westminster, 1960), 52.

41. Jo Ann Gardner, "Holy Aromas: Herbs and Spices of the Tabernacle," *The Herbarist* 76 (2010): 46.

42. Robert Louis Wilkin, *The First Thousand Years: A Global History of Christianity* (New Haven, CT: Yale University Press, 2012), 31.

43. See Minear, *Images of the Church in the New Testament*, 136–72.

44. Matt 10:41; 13:57; Mark 6:4; Luke 4:24; 13:33; John 4:44.

45. Matt 21:11, 26; Mark 6:15; 8:28; Luke 7:16, 39; 9:8, 19; John 6:14; 7:40; 9:17; Acts 3:22; 7:37.

46. We call the author of 1 and 2 Timothy and Titus, who writes in Paul's name but at least a generation after him, the Pastor because the three letters are pastoral in character.

47. Roger Beckwith, *Elders in Every City: The Origin and Role of the Ordained Ministry* (Waynesboro, GA: Paternoster, 2003). See also the helpful review by John T. Koenig in *Anglican Theological Review* 87, no. 3 (Summer 2005): 487–88.

48. R. Alistair Campbell, *The Elders: Seniority within Earliest Christianity* (Edinburgh: T&T Clark, 1994). See also E. P. Sanders, "Common Judaism and the Synagogue in the First Century," in *Jews, Christians and Polytheists in the Ancient Synagogue: Cultural Interaction during the Greco-Roman Period*, ed. Steven Fine, Baltic Studies in the History of Judaism (New York: Routledge, 1999), 1–15.

49. David W. Pao, "Waiters or Preachers: Acts 6:1-7 and the Lukan Table Fellowship Motif," *Journal of Biblical Literature* 130 (2011): 127–44.

50. Further on widows, see Jouette M. Bassler, "The Widows' Tale: A Fresh Look at 1 Tim 5:3-16," *Journal of Biblical Literature* 103 (1984): 23–41; Bonnie Bowman Thurston, *The Widows: A Women's Ministry in the Early Church* (Philadelphia: Fortress, 1989); Charlotte Methuen, "The 'Virgin Widow': A Problematic Social Role for the Early Church?" *Harvard Theological Review* 90, no. 3 (1997): 285–98.

4. Jesus' Hands and Feet

1. Ernst Käsemann, "The Theological Problem Presented by the Motif of the Body of Christ," in *Perspectives on Paul*, trans. Margaret Kohl (Philadelphia: Fortress, 1971), 104.

2. Eduard Schweizer, "*sōma*," in *Exegetical Dictionary of the New Testament*, ed. Horst Balz and Gerhard Schneider (Grand Rapids: Eerdmans, 1993; orig., 1983), 3:324, emphasis in the original.

3. Trans. Aubrey de Sélincourt, Loeb Classical Library (Cambridge, MA: Harvard University Press, 1960), 324–25.

4. Timothy L. Carter, "Looking at the Metaphor of Christ's Body in 1 Corinthians 12," in *Paul: Jew, Greek, and Roman*, ed. Stanley E. Porter, Pauline Studies 5 (Leiden: Brill, 2008), 94.

5. Plutarch, *Moralia*, trans. W. C. Helmbold, Loeb Classical Library (Cambridge, MA: Harvard University Press, 1939), 245–325.

6. Eduard Schweizer, "*sōma*," in *Theological Dictionary of the New Testament*, ed. Gerhard Kittel and Gerhard Friedrich (Grand Rapids: Eerdmans, 1964–76), 7:1032, 1036–41, 1055.

7. Margaret M. Mitchell, *Paul and the Rhetoric of Reconciliation: An Exegetical Investigation of the Language and Composition of 1 Corinthians* (Louisville, KY: Westminster John Knox, 1991), 157–64.

8. Paul S. Minear, *Images of the Church in the New Testament* (Philadelphia: Westminster, 1960), 173–220; Arland J. Hultgren, "The Church as the Body of Christ: Engaging an Image in the New Testament," *Word & World* 22 (2002): 124–32; David L. Bartlett, *Christology in the New Testament*, Core Biblical Studies (Nashville: Abingdon, 2017), 92–95.

9. Carter, "Looking at the Metaphor of Christ's Body," 110.

10. Matt 18:1-14; 19:13-15; 20:26-28 and parallels.

11. 1 Cor 5:3; 6:13, 15, 18, 20; 7:4, 34; 10:16; 11:27; 12:12, 15, 16, 18, 22, 23, 25; 15:35, 40.

12. Hultgren, "Church as the Body of Christ," 125–26.

13. David L. Bartlett, *Christology in the New Testament*, Core Biblical Studies (Nashville: Abingdon, 2017), 69–73.

14. Lincoln D. Hurst, *The Epistle to the Hebrews: Its Background of Thought*, SNTS Monograph Series 65 (Cambridge: Cambridge University Press, 1990), 71; Barnabas Lindars, *The Theology of the Letter to the Hebrews*, New Testament Theology (New York: Cambridge University Press, 1991), 12–13.

15. Minear, *Images of the Church*, 53–56.

16. See E. Elizabeth Johnson, "Ephesians," in *The Women's Bible Commentary*, ed. Carol Newsom, Sharon Ringe, and Jacqueline E. Lapsley, second ed. (Louisville, KY: Westminster John Knox, 2012), 576–80.

17. Renita J. Weems, *Battered Love: Marriage, Sex, and Violence in the Hebrew Prophets*, Overtures to Biblical Theology (Minneapolis: Augsburg Fortress, 1995).

18. An earlier Matthean parable similarly portrays competing groups of workers in a vineyard (Matt 20:1-16). A landowner hires one group of day laborers early in the morning, another group at noon, another group midafternoon, and another at the end of the day, agreeing to pay each group the same wage. When he pays them, the laborers hired first complain that they have worked longer than the last ones hired and the landowner replies that he does them no wrong since he pays what he promised to pay. The last hired may refer to Gentile Christians who are part of Matthew's church who may well be resented by the Jewish members who think of themselves as having always been part of God's covenant people and thus having priority.

19. Nils Alstrup Dahl, "The Parables of Growth," in *Jesus in the Memory of the Early Church* (Philadelphia: Augsburg, 1976).

20. Ryan P. Bonfiglio, personal communication, July 29, 2016.

21. Compare also Heb 13:20-21: "May the God of peace, who brought back the great shepherd of the sheep, our Lord Jesus, from the dead by

the blood of the eternal covenant, equip you with every good thing to do his will, by developing in us what pleases him through Jesus Christ."

22. Blake E. Wassell and Stephen R. Llewelyn, "Fishers of Humans,' The Contemporary Theory of Metaphor, and Conceptual Blending Theory," *Journal of Biblical Literature* 133, no. 3 (2014): 638.

23. Compare the parable of the weeds and the wheat (Matt 13:24-30).

24. Joshua R. Porter, "Leaven," in *HarperCollins Bible Dictionary*, ed. Paul L. Achtemeier et al. (New York: HarperCollins, 1996), 597.

25. Minear, *Images of the Church in the New Testament*, 105–35.

26. Obviously a riff on Jesus' words, "Where two or three are gathered in my name, I am there among them" (Matt 18:20 NRSV).

5. Water Is Thicker Than Blood

1. L. Michael White, *The Social Origins of Christian Architecture* (Valley Forge, PA: Trinity, 1996); Peter Oakes, *Reading Romans in Pompeii: Paul's Letter at Ground Level* (Minneapolis: Fortress, 2013).

2. John H. Elliott, "The Jesus Movement Was Not Egalitarian but Family-Oriented," *Biblical Interpretation* 11, no. 2 (2003): 173.

3. Further on this see E. Elizabeth Johnson, "'Who Is My Mother?' Family Values in the Gospel of Mark," in *Blessed One: Protestant Perspectives on Mary*, ed. Beverly R. Gaventa and Cynthia L. Rigby (Louisville, KY: Westminster John Knox, 2002), 32–46; Johnson, "Apocalyptic Family Values," *Interpretation* 56 (2002): 34–44; Johnson, "Life Together in the Household of God," in *Shaking Heaven and Earth: Essays in Honor of Walter Brueggemann and Charles B. Cousar*, ed. Christine Roy Yoder, Kathleen M. O'Connor, E. Elizabeth Johnson, and Stanley P. Saunders (Louisville, KY: Westminster John Knox, 2005), 89–103; Paul S. Minear, *Images of the Church in the New Testament* (Philadelphia: Westminster, 1960), 165–72.

4. For more, see Paul Veyne, *A History of Private Life*, vol. 1, *From Pagan Rome to Byzantium*, trans. Arthur Goldhammer (Cambridge, MA: Harvard University Press, 1992); Carolyn Osiek, RSCJ, "The Family in Early Christianity: 'Family Values' Revisited," *Catholic Biblical Quarterly* 58, no. 1 (1996): 1–24; David L. Balch and Carolyn Osiek, eds., *Early Christian Families in Context: An Interdisciplinary Dialogue* (Grand Rapids: Eerdmans, 2003).

5. Trans. H. Rackham, Loeb Classical Library (Cambridge, MA: Harvard University Press, 1932).

6. Warren Carter, *God in the New Testament*, Core Biblical Studies (Nashville: Abingdon, 2018).

7. *Abba* is the Aramaic word for "father." Jesus and his disciples spoke Aramaic, and remnants of that language appear occasionally elsewhere in the New Testament, which is written in Greek (e.g., *talitha koum*, "little girl, rise," Mark 5:41; *marana tha*, "Lord, come," 1 Cor 16:22). The fact that the same word, "father," occurs twice, first in Aramaic and then in Greek, suggests that the phrase "*Abba*, father" is liturgical language the Greek-speaking hearers of Paul's letters and Mark's Gospel already know. Liturgical language is famously slow to change. An analogy is when some contemporary church people still use archaic Elizabethan English when they pray the Lord's Prayer ("Our Father who art in heaven, hallowed be thy name").

8. There is inevitable theological risk in using only masculine images for God. As Mary Daly famously said, "If God is male, then the male is God" (*Beyond God the Father: Toward a Philosophy of Women's Liberation* [Boston: Beacon, 1973], 19). The androcentrism and misogyny of Western culture is persistently defended by recourse to the metaphor of God as father, which is why feminist and womanist Christians of the last quarter of the twentieth century worked diligently to recover the many and varied other ways to speak of God that do not absolutize gender as a defining characteristic.

9. The language of the specific inheritance varies. Sometimes it is the earth (Matt 5:5), eternal life (Matt 19:29; Mark 10:17; Luke 10:25; 18:18), God's kingdom (Matt 25:34; 1 Cor 6:9-10; 15:50; Gal 5:21; Eph 5:5).

the inheritance of the saints (Acts 20:32; Eph 1:18; Col 1:12; 3:24), the world (Rom 4:13), God's promises (Gal 3:18; Eph 1:11; Heb 6:12), redemption (Eph 1:14; Heb 1:14; 1 Pet 1:4), God's covenant (Heb 9:15), God's blessing (1 Pet 3:9), and the new heaven and new earth (Rev 21:7). Further on this, see Marianne Meye Thompson, *The Promise of the Father: Jesus and God in the New Testament* (Louisville, KY: Westminster John Knox, 2000).

10. My language here is shaped by Walter Brueggemann's "The Liturgy of Abundance, The Myth of Scarcity," *Christian Century* 116, no. 10 (Mar 24, 1999), available at https://www.christiancentury.org /article/2012-01/liturgy-abundance-myth-scarcity.

11. Quoted in W. V. Harris, "Child-Exposure in the Roman Empire," *The Journal of Roman Studies* 84 (1994): 4. To expose a child is to leave her in a public place where she will be found and taken in by someone.

12. See Wayne A. Meeks, "The Image of the Androgyne: Some Uses of a Symbol in Earliest Christianity," *History of Religions* 13, no. 3 (1974): 165–208.

13. The phrase "this cup" recalls the words of institution of the Lord's Supper in 1 Cor 11:25: "This cup is the new covenant in my blood. Do this, as often as you drink it, in remembrance of me" (NRSV cf. Matt 26:27; Mark 14:23; Luke 22:20; John 18:11; 1 Cor 10:16).

14. See Robert Louis Wilken, *The Christians as the Romans Saw Them*, second ed. (New Haven, CT: Yale University Press, 2003; orig., 1984), and Wayne A. Meeks, *The First Urban Christians: The Social World of the Apostle Paul* (New Haven, CT: Yale University Press, 1983), 173–74.

15. Joel Marcus makes the case that "those around him" in 3:21 means "his relatives" by pointing to similar usage of the phrase in the LXX and other Hellenistic literature (*Mark 1–8*, Anchor Bible 27 [New York: Doubleday, 2000], 270). The immediate literary context provides even stronger evidence that Mark has family in mind when he speaks of the people near to Jesus: the preceding paragraph enumerates the Twelve and describes their closeness to Jesus (3:13-19), in the following paragraph Jesus replaces his mother, brothers, and sisters with those

who do God's will (3:31-35), and the scene itself takes place "at home" (3:20).

16. The original is sufficiently ambiguous to bear all (or most) of the translation possibilities.

17. "When they heard it, his followers went out to calm it down, for they said it was out of control with enthusiasm" (Henry Wansbrough, "Mark III.21—Was Jesus Out of His Mind?" *New Testament Studies* 18, no. 2 [1972]: 233–35).

18. Johnson, "'Who Is My Mother?'" 36. Sociologists and anthropologists use the phrase *fictive kinship* to describe family relations that are modeled after but not created by legal (marriage, adoption, etc.) and biological (birth) bonds. A convenient and accessible introduction to the subject is K. C. Hanson, "BTB Readers Guide: Kinship," *Biblical Theology Bulletin* 24 (1994): 183–94.

19. See Matt 5:16, 45, 48; 6:1, 4, 6, 8, etc. The word "father" refers to God a total of 205 times in the New Testament.

20. For more on this, see Dierdre Good, *Jesus' Family Values* (New York: Seabury, 2006).

21. *Joseph and Asenath*, trans. C. Burchard, in *The Old Testament Pseudepigrapha*, ed. James H. Charlesworth (New York: Doubleday, 1985), 2:177–248. See also Raymond F. Collins, *The Many Faces of the Church: A Study in New Testament Ecclesiology* (New York: Crossroad, 2003), 16–29.

22. *Pirke Aboth: The Ethics of the Talmud, Sayings of the Fathers*, ed. and trans. R. Travers Herford (New York: Schocken, 1962).

23. Abraham J. Malherbe, *Paul and the Popular Philosophers* (Minneapolis: Fortress, 1989). Cf. Malherbe, "Ethics in Context: The Thessalonians and Their Neighbours," *Hervormde Teologiese Studies* 68, no. 1 (2012): 1–10.

24. Beverly Roberts Gaventa, "Apostles as Babes and Nurses in 1 Thessalonians 2:7" in *Faith and History: Essays in Honor of Paul W. Meyer*,

ed. John T. Carroll, Charles H. Cosgrove, and E. Elizabeth Johnson (Atlanta: Scholars Press, 1990), 193–207; Gaventa, "The Maternity of Paul: An Exegetical Study of Galatians 4:19," in *The Conversation Continues: Studies in Paul and John in Honor of J. Louis Martyn*, ed. Robert T. Fortna and Beverly Roberts Gaventa (Nashville: Abingdon, 1990), 189–201; Gaventa, "Mother's Milk and Ministry in 1 Corinthians 3," in *Theology and Ethics in Paul and His Interpreters: Essays in Honor of Victor Paul Furnish*, ed. Eugene H. Lovering Jr. and Jerry L. Sumney (Nashville: Abingdon, 1996), 101–13; Gaventa, "Our Mother St. Paul: Toward the Recovery of a Neglected Theme," in *A Feminist Companion to Paul*, ed. Amy-Jill Levine and Marianne Blickenstaff (London: T & T Clark, 2004), 85–97; Gaventa, *Our Mother Saint Paul* (Louisville, KY: Westminster John Knox, 2007).

25. Some manuscripts of verse 7 read "gentle" (*ēpioi*) and that is reflected in the CEB, NRSV, and the majority of modern translations. The more numerous manuscripts, though, read instead "infants" (*nēpioi*), as in the NIV, NET Bible, and Wycliffe Bible translations.

26. A wet nurse in antiquity is a slave woman who breastfeeds her master's children or a poor woman hired for the task. Popular opinion regards them as particularly loving and nurturing of their charges. If that is so, then Paul's description of himself as a wet nurse with her own children, not the master's children, ups the emotional ante. See Jennifer Houston McNeel, *Paul as Infant, and Nursing Mother: Metaphor, Rhetoric, and Identity in 1 Thessalonians 2:5-8*, Early Christianity and Its Literature 12 (Atlanta: Society of Biblical Literature Press, 2014).

27. For example, Abraham J. Malherbe, *The Letters to the Thessalonians*, Anchor Bible 32B (New Haven, CT: Yale University Press, 2004), 133–63.

28. Gaventa, *Our Mother Saint Paul*, 4–5.

29. M. Eugene Boring, *I and II Thessalonians: A Commentary* (Louisville, KY: Westminster John Knox, 2015), 86.

30. Matt 15:4; 19:19; Mark 7:10; 10:19; Luke 18:20.

31. Warren Carter demonstrates how Matthew similarly subverts conventional household order (*Households and Discipleship: A Study of Matthew 19–20*, Journal for the Study of the New Testament Supplement 103 [Sheffield, UK: Sheffield Academic Press, 1994]).

32. Although the people buried at Qumran were overwhelmingly male, there are a few women's and children's bodies as well, suggesting that at times there were also married people in the community.

33. Philo Judaea, a rough contemporary of Paul's, talks about the Therapeutae in *De vita contemplativa* 2–5, trans. F. H. Colson, Loeb Classical Library (Cambridge, MA: Harvard University Press, 1995; orig., 1941).

34. Jouette M. Bassler, "*Skeuos*: A Modest Proposal for Illuminating Paul's Use of Metaphor in 1 Thessalonians 4:4," in *The Social World of the First Christians: Essays in Honor of Wayne A. Meeks*, ed. L. Michael White and O. Larry Yarbrough (Philadelphia: Fortress, 1995), 53–66; E. Elizabeth Johnson, "A Modest Proposal in Context," in *The Impartial God: Essays in Honor of Jouette M. Bassler*, ed. Robert Foster (Sheffield, UK: Sheffield Phoenix Press, 2007), 232–45.

35. See E. Elizabeth Johnson, "Colossians," in *The Women's Bible Commentary*, ed. Carol Newsom, Sharon Ringe, and Cynthia Thompson (Louisville, KY: Westminster John Knox, 1992/1998), 437–39; Johnson, "Colossians," in *Harper's Bible Commentary*, rev ed (New York: Harper & Row, 2000), 1126–30; and Johnson, "Ephesians," in Newsom et al., *The Women's Bible Commentary*, 428–32.

36. A translation by Jeremiah Jones is available at "The Acts of Paul and Thecla," *From Jesus to Christ*, Frontline, https://www.pbs.org/wgbh/pages/frontline/shows/religion/maps/primary/thecla.html.

37. Johnson, "A Modest Proposal in Context," 242.

38. *Places in the Heart*, dir. by Robert Benton (1984; Twentieth Century Fox Home Entertainment, 2001 DVD).

Scripture Index

New Testament

Matthew

Mark

John

CPSIA information can be obtained
at www.ICGtesting.com
Printed in the USA
LVHW050837240620
658514LV00004B/4